COSTA DORADA
and BARCELONA

GW00692012

By the staff of Editions Berlitz

Berlitz Trademark Reg. U.S. Patent Office and other countries –
Marca Registrada. Library of Congress Catalog No. 76-21362.

Printed in Switzerland by Weber SA, Bienne

Revised edition 1982

Preface

A new kind of travel guide for the jet age. Berlitz has packed all you need to know about Spain's Costa Dorada and Barcelona into this compact and colourful book, one of an extensive series on the world's top tourist areas.

Like our phrase books and dictionaries, this book fits your pocket—in size and price. It also aims to fit your travel needs:

- It concentrates on your specific destination—the Costa Dorada and its capital, Barcelona—not an entire country.

- It combines easy reading with fast facts; what to see and do, where to shop, what to eat.

- An authoritative A-to-Z "blueprint", plus sections on how to get there and when to go, fills the back of the book.

- Easy-to-read maps in full colour of the major towns and regions pinpoint sights you'll want to see.

Let your travel agent help you choose a hotel.
Let a restaurant guide help you choose a good place to eat.
But to decide "What should we do today?", travel with Berlitz.

How to use this guide
If time is short, look for items to visit which are printed in bold type in this book, e.g. **Monumento a Colón.** Those sights most highly recommended are not only given in bold type but are also accompanied by our traveller symbol, e.g. **Sitges.**

Documentation: Ken Bernstein
Photography: Ken Welsh
We wish to thank the Spanish National Tourist Office, particularly Miss Mercedes Martín Bartolomé, for their valuable assistance.
4 Cartography: Falk-Verlag, Hamburg

Contents

Maps: Bird's-Eye View of Costa Dorada pp. 6–7, Costa Dorada pp. 18–19, Barcelona pp. 22–23, Barrio Gótico p. 25, La Rambla p. 30, Waterfront p. 39, Tarragona p. 55.
Photo: pp. 2–3, view from Parque Güell, Barcelona.

The Costa Dorada and Barcelona

The fine golden sand which gave the Costa Dorada its name extends almost without a break along more than 150 miles of this calm Mediterranean shore.

It begins just south of the more famous—and more crowded—Costa Brava and runs all the way down the coast of Catalonia to the delta of the mighty River Ebro. It encompasses a city as great as Barcelona and fishing villages too obscure to rate a post office. All along the coast, the swimming, boating and a bustling outdoor life continue uninterrupted under the dependable Spanish sun—until the moon and stars take over with the nightlife.

Sheer holiday fun is just one part of the Costa Dorada's invitation. This is a land of magnificent ancient churches and castles. Inland, beyond the vineyards, you can visit the

E S P A Ñ A

Ebro

Cambrils   Tarragona

S. Carlos
de la Rápita

Villanu
y Gelt

COSTA DORADA

F. Biegel

unique mountain monastery of Montserrat—or less celebrated but unsurpassed treasures of architecture and faith. And wherever you may find yourself along the Costa Dorada, you'll sense the dynamism of Catalonia.

Spaniards in general may cherish their siesta, but the Catalan people can take it or (like the big department stores) leave it. Most Spaniards keep their women at home; in Catalonia, women enter the professions and direct traffic. Spaniards may dance the fiery flamenco; Catalans hold hands for the stately, measured *sardana*.

The people are bilingual. They speak Catalan, a derivative of Latin, as well as (and often better than) the official language of Spain, Castilian. They are more adept with foreign languages than other Spaniards. In the Middle Ages, the Catalans ruled a great sweep of the Mediterranean, including at one time or another Sicily, Sardinia, Corsica and parts of Greece. The language and culture which flourished in those imperial times still bind the Barcelona industrialist to the San Pol fisherman and the Amposta rice farmer.

Modern Catalonia has produced an inordinately bounti-

ful crop of original artists, such as Joan Miró and Salvador Dalí and, something of an adopted son, Picasso. But centuries earlier, brilliant Catalan architects designed stunning Romanesque churches, decorated with frescoes full of movement and colour. With a bit of time, a tourist can see the best of everything, ancient and modern, either housed in the Costa Dorada's museums or on the spot.

The metropolis of Catalonia, Barcelona, is a vital and very European city of flower stalls and tree-lined boulevards. The glory of its medieval architecture complements the audacity of its modern buildings. The citizens, renowned for their industriousness, work hard in 19th-century factories with huge brick chimney-stacks, or on the docks, or behind the counters of a proliferation of banks. They read more books, see more operas, and, inexplicably, go to more bullfights than the people of any other Spanish city.

The other major port on this coast, Tarragona, was a provincial capital of imperial Rome. Imaginative landscaping and dramatic floodlighting at night enliven its archaeological splendours. And, in a city said to have been converted to Christianity by St. Paul himself, the cathedral—begun in the 12th century—fills the visitor with a sense of awe.

On the political map of Spain, the Costa Dorada belongs to Barcelona and Tarragona provinces. (Lérida and Gerona are Catalonia's other two provinces.) In this important wine-producing district, the carafe on your table will probably be a tasty local vintage. Fishing is also a big industry, so you can be certain of fresh-from-the-net seafood. Other principal industrial activities are textile manufacture and—obviously—tourism.

The Catalans may be realists and individualists, but they are wild about singing in choirs and playing in bands and dancing the graceful *sardana*. A more eccentric aspect of their folklore is an earnest enthusiasm for climbing upon each others' shoulders to create dangerously swaying pyramids. Teams of trained castle-makers *(castellers)* travel the countryside for contests; the newspapers run articles; and, of course, the peculiar music of Catalan woodwind instruments accompanies each climax.

You'll like the cooking. From typical Catalan farm soup (loaded with sausage, beans, and a slice of meat-loaf) to nuts (local almonds, of course), the food is good and wholesome.

And before your holiday ends, you'll want to squeeze in some shopping. Local artisans and regional factories produce gifts and souvenirs both corny and sophisticated, shockingly cheap or, alas, hopelessly expensive. In a word, something for every taste.

In a Barcelona square, Catalans hold hands to dance the sardana.

A Brief History

Catalonia's long road from colony to imperial power and back to provincial status zigzags through extremes of idealism and cruelty, triumph and disaster. Characters as colourful as the Caesars, Charlemagne, and Ferdinand and Isabella left their mark on its history.

So did a 9th-century warrior named Wilfred the Hairy (Wifredo el Velloso), Catalonia's first-ever hero, who threw his noble if shaggy support behind a Frankish king called Charles the Bald. Charles was trying to expel the Moors, a recurring project in the Middle Ages. When Hairy Wilfred fell wounded, the legend goes, the king asked what reward he desired. The request—independence for Barcelona—was granted. The year was 878.

But to begin at the beginning takes us far into prehistoric times. Paleolithic and Neolithic relics have turned up in Catalonia. While little is known of those early people, we are however sure that Phoenicians and Greeks brought commerce and culture to Catalonia; and the Carthaginians are said to have given Barcelona its original name, Barcino, in honour of General Hamilcar Barca, father of the legendary Hannibal.

In the 2nd Punic War (3rd century B.C.), the Romans defeated Carthage and ruled Iberia for the next six centuries. Spain gave birth to four Roman emperors. One of the capitals of the Roman empire was Tarragona, then called Tarraco. All over Catalonia, from the seashore to lonely mountaintops, the stamp of Rome remains: walls and roadways, villas and monuments, vineyards and the Catalan language, an expressive descendant of Latin.

By the 5th century A.D., Rome's grip had slackened and Spain was overrun by Vandals and Visigoths. The next in-

Aqueduct near Tarragona recalls Catalonia's role in Roman empire.

vasion began in 711, when Moorish forces from Africa assailed the Iberian peninsula. Muslim civilization was imposed, but the Christian efforts to reconquer Spain never ceased. The subsequent Moorish influence on Christian Spanish art and architecture, was, nonetheless, profound.

An early but indecisive defeat of the Moors was the recapture of Barcelona by Charlemagne's forces. Catalonia paid generously for its liberation, becoming a Frankish dependency called the Spanish March. Then came our heroic Count Wilfred the Hairy, who earned Barcelona its freedom.

Catalonia's Golden Age

In the Middle Ages, Catalonia prospered commercially, poli-

tically and intellectually. Count Ramón Berenguer I of Barcelona drew up a sort of constitution, the *Usatges,* in 1060. Ramón Berenguer III (1096–1131) turned Catalonia towards imperial enterprises; he formed a union with an independent Provence (the languages are very similar) and established trade relations with Italy. Ramón Berenguer IV (1131–62) married a princess of Aragon, a brilliant expansionist tactic which created a joint kingdom of great substance. The count of Barcelona became king of Aragon, and "greater Catalonia" flourished.

Jaime I (James the Conqueror) dislodged the Moors from their stubborn hold on the Balearic Islands, installing in their stead Christianity and Catalan law. His son, Pedro III the Great, through military action and a few twists of fate, added the throne of Sicily to the dynasty's collection. By the 14th century, Catalonia's fortunes had soared to breathtaking heights, with the addition of two dukedoms in Greece, the seizure of Sardinia, and the annexation of Corsica. For a time the kingdom of Catalonia was Power No. 1 in **12** the entire Mediterranean.

This was the era, too, of great art and architecture—original designs for churches with vast naves and tall, slim columns and the striking sculptures and paintings which glorified them. And this was a heyday for the language. Ramón Llull of Majorca (1235–1315), known as Raimundus Lullus in Latin, saint and scholar, enhanced medieval culture in

Catalan. At the same time, Catalonian cartographers, especially Majorcans, were drawing the maps that were to guide the first great navigators on their journeys beyond the known horizon.

The next Catalonian figure to make history was Ferdinand (Ferran II in Catalan), who married Isabella of Castile and became Ferdinand V of Spain.

ages of discovery proved disastrous for Catalonia. The Mediterranean lost much of its importance as a trading zone, while the south-western ports of Cadiz and Seville won the franchise for the rich transatlantic business.

Giant effigies (opposite) *honour Ferdinand and Isabella. In Barcelona port, a replica of Columbus' ship.*

Ferdinand and Isabella, known as the Catholic Monarchs, conquered the last Moorish bastion, Granada. They also took joint credit for two other big events in 1492: they ordered the expulsion of Spain's Jews, and they sponsored Columbus on his voyage of discovery to America. Ironically, the Columbus project and other voy-

Times of Troubles

Seventeenth-century Catalonia was a troubled land, rebelling against Philip IV of Spain, putting itself under the protection of the king of France. Violent struggles went on for a dozen years. Finally a besieged Barcelona surrendered. Catalonia renewed its allegiance to the Spanish crown, but man- **13**

aged to preserve its treasured local laws.

But all was lost in the War of the Spanish Succession, in which Catalonia again demonstrated its marked difference from the rest of Spain and joined the wrong side. With the triumph of the Bourbon king Philip V in 1714, Barcelona was overrun. Official punishment followed, including the dismissal of the Catalonian parliament and the banning of the Catalan language from official use. Striking historical parallels were to follow the Spanish Civil War of 1936–39.

In the second half of the 18th century, Charles III—usually characterized as an enlightened despot—rescued Catalonia from its slump, opening up the region's ports to the very profitable Latin-American trade. He also had a visionary idea for a superport on the edge of the Ebro Delta, but the metropolis of San Carlos de la Rápita (see page 63) never amounted to much more than an extravagant mirage.

For Catalonia as well as the rest of Spain, the 19th century seemed to be just one war after another, starting with the War of the Third Coalition in 1805 and ending with the Spanish-American War of 1898. Both were disasters. In the first, the British, under Nelson, destroyed the Spanish and French fleets at Trafalgar. In the last, Spain lost its key remaining colonies—Cuba, Puerto Rico and the Philippines.

Lauros-Giraudon

After finding America, Columbus sailed triumphantly to Barcelona.

Thirty-three years after the empire faded away, King Alfonso XIII went into exile, as Republicans gained control in several Spanish cities. National elections later in 1931 favoured the Republicans, who advocated socialist and anti-clerical policies. As conservative resistance began to crystallize, Catalonia was proclaimed an autonomous republic. This was the first time in more than two centuries that home rule had been achieved.

The Civil War

But confusion and disorder were growing in Spain. The conflict between left and right became more irreconcilable. Spain's youngest general, Francisco Franco, came to the head of a military insurrection. The whole world watched the three-year struggle; outside forces helped to prolong it. The Nationalists—Franco and the Falangists and Monarchists—could call upon the tanks and planes of Germany and Italy. The Republicans—a shaky coalition of Socialists, Communists and Anarchists—received help from Moscow and the volunteer International Brigade.

Military reverses forced the Republicans to move their capital from Valencia to Barcelona in late 1937 where there had already been an outbreak of bitter fighting between two factions of the Republican side, Anarchists and Communists. There followed repeated bombings of Barcelona by Italian planes based on Majorca and a year of hardship for the population. The city fell at last in January, 1939, and Catalonia was reabsorbed into Spain—four provinces out of the nation's 50. Within two months, the Civil War, in which not far from half a million Spaniards were killed, was over.

Modern Times

Spain's neutrality in the Second World War enabled it to heal its wounds. In 1955, the country was admitted to the U.N. The subsequent tourist invasion had profound effects on the economy and on the people. On Franco's death in 1975, King Juan Carlos I was crowned. In spite of big problems, Catalonia and the Basque country have moved towards greater autonomy, and democratic structures have been evolved; Spain is now fully integrated into the mainstream of Western European life.

Where to Go

Maresme, meaning a low-lying coastal region susceptible to flooding. The beaches go on for mile after mile of ideal sand and clear sea, with impressive mountains in the distance. Every fifth hilltop seems to be occupied by a castle or at least a medieval watch-tower. These relics are so common that only the best preserved or most historic are signposted.

The Coast North of Barcelona

The Costa Brava is known for its rugged cliffs and small inlets, but the Costa Dorada is downright cowardly. Rarely is the lie of the land more daring than a few miles of broad sand beaches nuzzling against a clear, gentle sea.

Let's begin by a survey of the coastline, first heading north-east from Barcelona up to the Costa Brava frontier.

The voyage starts with BA-DALONA (population 210,000), a last reminder of big-city rush and industrial necessities.

Beyond Badalona the countryside gradually takes on a more rural cast. The towns, no longer sprawling suburbs, have self-contained identities. The entire area is known as the

Costa Dorada consists of miles of lazy beaches interspersed with towns as fair as Sitges (opposite).

The first real beach centres, in a countryside noted for flower-growing, are MASNOU and PREMIÁ DE MAR. These beaches run right alongside the railway line.

This was the first railway in Spain, built under British technical direction and inaugurated in 1848 between Barcelona and MATARÓ, now an industrial city of about 80,000. It's all work and no play in Mataró; a tourist with a tan attracts stares from the pale local residents. Mataró was called Iluro by the ancient Romans, who left many priceless sculptures and mosaics. Most of these archaeological finds went into the municipal museum, which was shut down in 1975 when more than 200 items were found to be missing. The museum curator resigned.

CALDETAS, also known as Caldas de Estrach (or Caldes d'Estrac in Catalan*), is an appealing old town with villas set among the pines on its hillsides. The Romans bathed in

its fine 102° Fahrenheit mineral waters; so do some of today's visitors. This unspoiled spa also has plenty of seashore.

Since the 16th century, when the village church was built, ARENYS DE MAR has been a seafaring town. Nowadays the fishing fleet is greatly outnumbered by pleasure boats; Arenys's impressive modern marina makes it an international sailing and yachting centre. The town itself climbs from the shore along a stately tree-lined main street. The parish church contains a sumptuous baroque altarpiece which tourists may appreciate better by depositing money in a coin

---

* Many place names in Catalonia create spelling problems. In this book we avoid pedantic or nationalistic passions and spell the towns as they're most often listed on road signs and local maps.

18

slot to switch on a spotlight.

SAN POL, a fishing village with charm, has only about 2,000 inhabitants. Aside from some sports facilities and a few quiet hotels San Pol makes little effort to share its several beaches with outsiders. Unlike many a coastal town, it has been able to preserve its character.

CALELLA, sometimes known as Calella de la Costa or Calella de Mar, bustles with tourist development. Eleven-floor blocks of flats and more than 80 hotels house the thousands of visitors who converge here for what the local tourist board calls "cosmopolitan gaiety". Among distinguishing characteristics are a white lighthouse atop a knoll at the south edge of town; an 18th-century church; and a tree-shaded promenade along a very wide sand beach. Its many streets of souvenir shops, bars and restaurants prove Calella's importance as one of the coast's most popular international resorts.

From here to MALGRAT, the Costa Dorada extends for miles of almost empty beaches. Camping sites take advantage of some choice stretches; but the flat countryside consists mainly of sea and sand. Malgrat itself is an undistinguished industrial town of 10,000 with a small, dusty main square, and 3 miles of beach, but it does provide the ingredients for an economical seaside holiday.

The Costa Dorada runs out just beyond Malgrat. Officially the Costa Brava begins on the other side of the River Tordera. The actual boundary, of scant **19** interest to anyone but a mapmaker or tax collector, is a river-bed a couple of hundred yards wide. In summer it's normally bone dry and desolate. In winter, though, water rushes down from the Sierra de Montseny in search of the sea. That's when the Tordera turns into a raging flood. It has been known to overflow its banks and even wash away a bridge or two.

Tourists along this stretch of the Costa Dorada are in a good position to sign up for sea excursions beyond the jurisdictional frontiers. The boats normally call at such celebrated resorts as Blanes, Lloret, Tossa and San Feliú de Guixols. The Costa Brava's spectacular scenery, admired from the sea, justifies its claim to world renown.

Barcelona

Catalonia's capital is a very big city with muscle and brains. Close on two million people live within the boundaries of this centre of banking, publishing and smoky heavy industry. Another million live in the surrounding metropolitan area.

Its main attractions for visitors are renowned—the mighty cathedral, the port, gracious promenades and distinguished museums. You have to be alert for the smaller delights: a noble patio hidden in a slum, a tiled park bench moulded to the anatomy, a street-light fixture lovingly worked in iron, a sculpted gargoyle sneering down from medieval eaves.

The lively people of Barcelona know how to make money. They spend it on flowers and football, music and books, and gooey pastries for their children. They enjoy the bullfights and dancing in the street. They go to gourmet snack-bars and sexy floor-shows, and wear formal evening dress to the opera house.

In the Middle Ages Barcelona was the capital of a surprisingly influential Catalonia. Thirteenth-century Barcelona, ruling distant cities of the Mediterranean, was building big ships in what is today the Maritime Museum, and living by Europe's first code of sea law.

The next great era, economically and artistically, came with late 19th-century industrialization. Politically, the 20th century witnessed a brief revival. In 1931, Barcelona became the capital of an autonomous Catalan Republic, that came to an end in 1939 when General Franco's Nationalist troops triumphed. Although a province in name, Barcelona's spirit has not changed. The capital of Wilfred the Hairy and James the Conqueror remains an outward-looking, eminently European city.

El Barrio Gótico

To walk through 15 centuries of history, through the so-called *Barrio Gótico* (Gothic Quarter), we start, arbitrarily, at the city's present-day hub,

"Aerial ropeway" over Barcelona's port offers panorama of lively city.

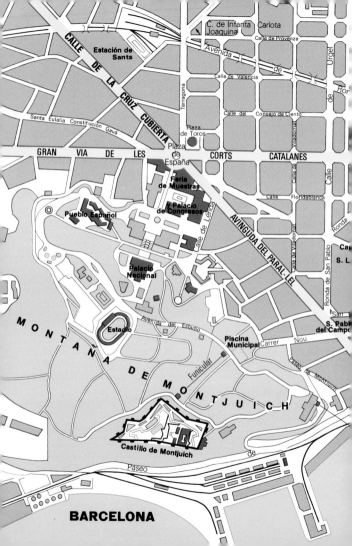

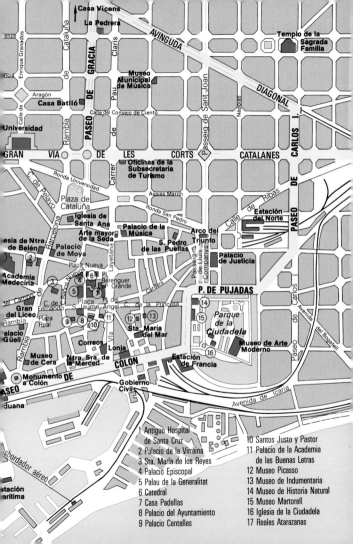

Casa Vicens
La Pedrera
AVINGUDA
Templo de la
Sagrada
Familia
DIAGONAL
Enrique Granados
Clarís
de
GRACIA
PASEO DE
Pau
Claris
Museo
Municipal
de Música
Calle de
Aragón
Casa Batlló
Calle del Consejo de Ciento
Passeig de Sant Joan
Nápoles
CARLOS
Universidad
Rambla
DE
GRAN VIA DE LES CORTS CATALANES
C. de Pelayo
Oficinas de la
Subsecretaría
de Turismo
Ronda Universidad
de Ribas
Estación
del Norte
Ausias March
Plaza de
Cataluña
Ronda San Pedro
Barcelona
Iglesia de
Santa Ana
Palacio de la
Música
Arco del
Triunfo
Palacio
de Justicia
Iglesia de Ntra.
de Belén
Arte mayor
de la Seda
S. Pedro
de las Puellas
Palacio
de Moya
Plaza Nueva
Academia
Medecina
P. Berenguer
Grande
Carders
P. DE PUJADAS
Gran
del Liceo
C. de
Plaza
Real
Plaza
S. Jaume
Angel
C. de la Princesa
Parque
de la
Ciudadela
Museo de Arte
Moderno
Palacio
Güell
Sta. María
del Mar
Correos
Museo
de Cera
Lonja
Ntra. Sra.
de la Merced
COLON
Estación
de Francia
Monumento
a Colón
Gobierno
Civil
PASEO DE
Avenida de Icaria
Duana
Estación
Marítima

1 Antiguo Hospital
  de Santa Cruz
2 Palacio de la Virreina
3 Sta. María de los Reyes
4 Palacio Episcopal
5 Palau de la Generalitat
6 Catedral
7 Casa Padellas
8 Palacio del Ayuntamiento
9 Palacio Centelles

10 Santos Justo y Pastor
11 Palacio de la Academia
   de las Buenas Letras
12 Museo Picasso
13 Museo de Indumentaria
14 Museo de Historia Natural
15 Museo Martorell
16 Iglesia de la Ciudadela
17 Reales Atarazanas

the **Plaza de Cataluña** (Catalonia Square). Most of the bus, metro and railway lines converge here. Day and night, the traffic swirls around this paved and flower-bedded island.

At the south-eastern edge of the plaza begins a short but important street intriguingly named **Puerta del Angel** (Gate of the Angel). As it descends from Plaza de Cataluña, the

Barrio Gótico: delights of medieval architecture at every turn.

street narrows; for most hours of the day, it's a pedestrians-only sanctuary, with convenient benches for tired feet.

Avenida de la Puerta del Angel leads to **Plaza Nueva** (New Square), not new at all. In the

13th century, this was a major market area. Among the commodities sold here were slaves. Incongruously, the modern building of the College of Architects overlooks this ancient square. At first glance, you might think the façades of the College had been decorated by children. On second glance, you'd be right in guessing that the author of these huge graffiti could be none other than Pablo Picasso, who contributed these sketches on the theme of Catalan folklore.

From here the spires of the cathedral are already in sight. We'll take a closer look shortly. But first, notice the two stone towers straight ahead. Known as the Bishop's Gate, they were part of the 4th-century Roman wall, raised higher eight centuries later.

Walk between the towers, that is, between the Bishop's Palace and the Archdeacon's House, and you will immediately feel the other-worldliness of Barcelona's Gothic Quarter. Take a look at the Romanesque patio of the Bishop's Palace, the first of many majestic courtyards to be seen in Barcelona. Very little connection could be claimed between the elegance of these columned precincts and the idea of a Spanish patio of whitewashed stucco.

The patio of the **Casa del Arcediano** (the Archdeacon's House) is more intimate and appealing, with its slim palm tree and moss-covered fountain. The 11th-century building was restored in the early 16th century.

And so to the **Catedral de Santa Eulalia** (St. Eulalia Cathedral), dedicated to a legendary local girl who was tortured and executed for her fervent Christian faith in the 4th century.

The cathedral's construction was begun at the end of the 13th century and lasted for about 150 years. At the end of the 19th century, new work was undertaken thanks to a subsidy from a rich industrialist. Some critics complain that he spoiled the pure Catalan Gothic effect. But don't worry about the critics. Come back one night when the delicate spires are illuminated and light inside glows through the stained-glass windows. It's a pulse-quickening sight by any standards.

The interior of the cathedral is laid out in classic Catalan Gothic form, with three aisles neatly engineered to produce

an effect of grandeur and uplift.

Look into the side chapels, with their precious paintings and sculptures. In the chapel of St. Benedict, the lifelike **Altarpiece of the Transfiguration** is the work of a great 15th-century Catalan artist, Bernat Martorell.

The **choir,** in the geometric centre of the cathedral, con-

1 Palacio Episcopal
2 Casa del Arcediano
3 Catedral
4 Palau de la Generalitat
5 Ayuntamiento

6 Palacio Real Mayor (Museo Federico Marés)
7 Capilla Real de Santa Agueda
8 Casa Padellas

centrates dazzling sculptural intricacies. The 15th-century German sculptor Michael Lochner carved the splendid **25** canopies over the choir pews.

A wide stairway leads beneath the high altar to the crypt of the aforementioned St. Eulalia. Notice the rogue's gallery of small stone-carved heads around the stairway and entry arch. The saint's carved alabaster sarcophagus dates from 1327.

For a change to a cheery atmosphere, step into the

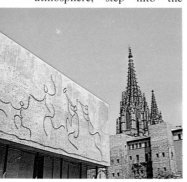

cloister, a 15th-century Gothic classic. All cloisters are supposed to be tranquil, and so is this—except for the half dozen argumentative geese who rule the roost here, as have their ancestors for centuries.

The **Museo de la Catedral** (Cathedral Museum) displays religious paintings and sculpture from the 14th century onwards.

Before leaving the cathedral, step into the **Capilla de Santa Lucía** (St. Lucy's Chapel), a spartan 13th-century sanctuary built by the bishop whose sepulchre is on view. Notice the 13th- and 14th-century tombstones in the floor. Every step, as they say, touches a bit of history.

Now a few other highlights near the cathedral in the Gothic Quarter:

Museo Federico Marés (Federico Marés Museum). An ambitious collection of statues from the 10th century on.

Museo de Historia de la Ciudad (Museum of the History of the City). The average visitor may choose to neglect Barcelona's old maps and documents, collected in this pleasant palace, but the scene below ground is unforgettable. Subterranean passages follow the admirable tracks of Roman civilization. Houses, waterworks, statues and ceramics have been excavated. In search of ballast for the ancient city's defensive towers, they threw in anything at hand including tombs, plaques and upside-down columns. Now archaeologists are tunnelling under the very cathedral to uncover relics of the Visigoths.

The museum faces Barcelona's most historic square, **Plaza del Rey** (King's Square). According to unconfirmed tradition, Columbus was received on this very spot when he returned a hero from his first voyage to the New World. Ferdinand and Isabella, the Catholic Monarchs, may have sat on the great steps of **Salón del Tinell** (Tinell Hall). They're shown thus, sitting in a famous stylized painting in which American Indians brought back by Columbus fairly swoon with ecstasy at the sight of their new masters.

Cathedral tower looms over façade by Picasso. Plaza del Rey (below) is a splendid medieval ensemble.

Whether or not Columbus climbed the ceremonial stairs, Tinell Hall would have been a fine spot for his "welcome home" reception. Built in the 14th century, it consists of one immense room with a wood-panelled ceiling supported by six arches. Above the hall is an architectural afterthought of the mid-16th century, the **Torre del Rey Martín** (King Martin's Lookout Tower). This curious accumulation of porticoed galleries rises five storeys above the hall—just the place to mount a spy-glass to see the sea.

The square is also bounded by the **Capilla de Santa Agueda** (Chapel of St. Agatha), a 13th-century royal church with a slender tower. The far side of the chapel, facing the modern city, rests on the ancient Roman wall. You can see it all in detail from the **Plaza Ramón Berenguer el Grande,** a sort of sunken garden right against the chapel and the wall.

The **Generalitat** (provincial council) on the north side of Plaça Sant Jaume is the home of Catalonia's parliament. This ceremonious 15th-century structure hides a surprise or two: the overpowering ornamentation of St. George's Room and an upstairs patio with orange trees.

Across the square, the **Ayuntamiento** (city hall) is even older. A sumptuous highlight of this 14th-century political centre is the **Salón del Consejo de Ciento** (Chamber of the Council of One Hundred), restored to its original glory worthy of any parliament.

But medieval life in Barcelona was not all pomp and majesty. Just to the west of the Generalitat, narrow streets with names like Call and Baños Nuevos mark the ancient Jewish Quarter. In the 11th, 12th and 13th centuries, it was a centre of philosophy, poetry and science. The Jews were money-lenders, also, and financed King Jaime I in his Mediterranean conquests. In 1391, as anti-semitic passions gripped Spain, the Barcelona ghetto was sacked. More than 300 Jews died within an hour. In 1395, one of the ghetto's synagogues was converted into what is now the Iglesia de San Jaime (Church of St. James), just around the corner from the city hall.

La Rambla, relaxed but always dynamic, charms young and old.

La Rambla

Barcelona's best-known promenade, La Rambla, descends gradually but excitingly from Plaza de Cataluña to the port, a distance of about a mile. Like the women of Barcelona, La Rambla may not be very beautiful, but it's full of life, self-assurance and charm. Almost every visitor succumbs to the attraction of this boulevard, thronged day and night with a fascinating crowd of people, animals and things. When you can't walk another inch along the undulating paving designs in the central walkway, watch the parade of the passing crowd from an outdoor café or rent a chair from a concessionaire.

Every couple of cross-streets the Rambla's character subtly changes. So does its official name, five times in all—but that needn't concern us. It may explain why the Rambla is often referred to in the plural as Las Ramblas.

The start of the Rambla at the Plaza de Cataluña ought to be its most elegant area, but this is not really so. The air of animation here might baffle or mislead an outsider. Those groups of men spiritedly ar-

guing are not forming political parties or disputing dogma. They are football fans conducting post-mortems after a match.

Here, too, you can buy a newspaper, magazine or book from the international choice displayed at the news-stands. The Rambla is also the kind of place where you can buy a lottery ticket or one cigarette from a very small businessman.

Not far beyond the Hyde Park Corner of football experts there used to be a university centre. In the 16th and 17th centuries, students congregated here; the name — Rambla de los Estudios — remains.

The huge old **Iglesia de Belén** (Church of Bethlehem), on the right, looks as if it might be an important attraction. But not in this city of so many truly exceptional churches, big and small.

You can buy a bird or a monkey along here, or just stand and stare at one of many stands dealing in canaries, doves, parrots and pigeons. Beyond the bird zone come the flower kiosks with their year-round colour: local carnations, Canary Islands bird-of-paradise flowers, and potted cacti.

The Palacio de la Virreina

(a reference to the Spanish vicereine in 18th-century Peru) is more than just a graceful building. It houses the **Colección Cambó** (Cambó Collection), a jewel of a museum. A Catalan named Francisco Cambó (who died in Buenos Aires in 1947) assembled 50 paintings by the greatest Italian, French, Spanish and Dutch artists. This is one museum without disappointments or needless detours; every item is priceless. Other floors of the palace are used for topical exhibitions.

The **mercado de San José,** one of those classic iron-covered and colonnaded markets of the 19th century, faces the Rambla. You have to wander among the eye-catching displays to appreciate the wealth of fresh fruit and vegetables, meat and seafood available here. The fish are lovingly laid out on crushed ice.

Just behind the market, in the Plaza del Doctor Fleming (honouring the discoverer of penicillin), a profession of bygone centuries endures. Four men sit in adjacent small booths, filling the ancient role of scribes. With increasing literacy among the population they now offer a more sophisticated range of services—typ- **31** ing business letters, translating, expediting official forms. But they're still known to ghost-write a love letter or two.

A further detour from the market goes to the **Hospital de la Santa Cruz,** now a formidable combination of buildings including the Library of Catalonia and the 18th-century Royal Academy of Medicine and Surgery. See the old operating theatre lit by a great crystal chandelier. A pilgrims' hospital stood here from the beginning of the 13th century.

Back on the Rambla, the main entrance to the **Gran Teatro del Liceo,** Spain's leading opera house, almost goes unnoticed. Inside the theatre, however, all is calculatedly ostentatious. When it opened in the mid-19th century this velvet-and-gilt opera house was considered the world's best.

Carrer Nou de la Rambla and the Rambla itself make up the unofficial boundaries of a district of ill repute called the **Barrio Chino** (Chinatown). Prostitution was outlawed in Spain in 1956 but you'd never know it in this part of Barcelona. From midday to dawn the narrow old streets call to mind the darkest corners of Marseilles.

Travels with Sancho

An early tourist, Don Quixote de la Mancha, had never seen the sea until he visited Barcelona. The most universal fictional hero of all time also toured a publishing house.

In chapter 60 of Book Two of Cervantes' immortal novel, Quixote sums up the rough-tough atmosphere of 16th-century Barcelona, where "they hang outlaws and bandits 20 by 20 and 30 by 30". Running into the macabre aftermath of a mass execution in a forest, Quixote anticipates an old joke and says, "I reckon I must be near Barcelona".

On the edge of this tawdry zone stands a fine ancient church called **San Pablo del Campo** (St. Paul-in-the-Fields). The stone carvings are nearly a thousand years old. Step into the dark Romanesque interior, reconstructed in the 12th century. The arches surrounding the small cloister have unique Moorish-inspired designs.

One more diversion, on the opposite side of the Rambla: the **Plaza Real** (Royal Square) is Barcelona's most perfectly proportioned square. Try to see it on a Sunday morning, when the stamp- and coin-collectors turn the arcaded square into a market-place. Watch grim-faced professionals, equipped with their own magnifying glasses and tweezers, facing each other across coin trays or stamp albums like champion chess players.

Toward the bottom of the promenade a uniformed usher and an identically clothed wax effigy solicit business for Barcelona's **Museo de Cera** (Wax Museum), just across the street.

Symmetrical arcades and tall palm trees add harmony to Plaza Real.

Women in white smocks operate Daguerrotype-style cameras to sell instant memories to newly-arrived sailors and provincials. And a talkative mystery woman gathers a crowd as she coaxes a small bird to tell fortunes by choosing a slip of paper from a pack of prophesies.

The Rambla leads on down to the Columbus monument and the port (see p. 37). Whether you stay in the shade of the tall plane trees on the promenade or cross the traffic to window-shop along the edges of the street (where you can buy anything from a guitar to a deep-sea diving-bell), you'll want to walk the Rambla from beginning to end and back again. For better or worse, this is surely where it's all happening.

Montjuich

It's pronounced mon-ZHWEEK, and whether you reach it by foot, taxi, bus or funicular, you could spend a whole day there and not see everything you ought to.

Montjuich is a modest mountain less than 700 feet high. Until relatively recently, it had **34** only military significance. But Barcelona's World Exhibition of 1929 saw hundreds of buildings planted upon its hillsides. The best are still there.

Montjuich begins, more or less officially, where the exhibition began—at Plaza de España, a huge and frightening traffic roundabout. Facing each other at great distance across the plaza are a bullring (one of two in Barcelona) and the town airline terminal. From here, you can look up the hillside, past the commercial exhibition grounds to a great **fountain,** one of Barcelona's prides. On weekend and holiday evenings, the waters are inventively illuminated. The central jet rises as high as 165 feet; water roars up at 642 gallons per second.

Looming above all this, with a dome reminiscent of the U.S. Capitol building in Washington, is a palace built as recently as 1929—for the Barcelona World Fair. Architecturally, the Palacio Nacional won't win any prizes for originality, but it houses the **Museo de Arte de Cataluña** (Museum of Art of Catalonia), one of the world's greatest collections of medieval art. Sixty-eight exhibition halls follow chronological order in this exceptionlly well organized museum; maps of the museum are posted n every room to help you find your way. The only problem might be linguistic, for explanations are solely in Spanish and Catalan.

The 10th- and 11th-century Catalan religious paintings bear a striking resemblance to ancient Byzantine icons. See the beautiful 12th-century wood carvings from church altars, and magnificent frescoes of the same period, rescued from crumbling old churches.

Most conducted tours of Barcelona stop at **Pueblo Español,** a five-acre exhibition of Spanish art and architecture, in the form of an artificial village designed to show off the charms and styles of Spain's regions in super-concentration.

Another leftover from the World Exhibition of 1929, the Palace of Graphic Arts has been turned into the **Museo Arqueológico** (Archaeological Museum). The prehistoric items come mostly from Catalonia and the Balearic Islands. Many Greek and Roman relics come from Ampurias, the Costa Brava town first settled by the Phoenicians in the 6th century B.C. There are also architectural displays from Barcelona's Roman days.

The **Museo Etnológico y Colonial** (Ethnological Museum) of Montjuich is devoted to specimens gathered by expeditions to exotic far-off places.

The newest museum on the mountain, opened in 1975, goes under the unwieldy name of **Fundació Joan Miró – Centre d'Estudis d'Art Contemporani.**

Charming old Spanish-style street transplanted to Pueblo Español.

This complex of original concrete and glass buildings is a tribute to the great Catalan artist Joan Miró, and the intense Catalanism of the place extends to the titles of the works, given in Catalan and occasionally also in French, but never in Spanish. What **35** with the bright architecture and the riot of Miró paintings, sculptures, drawings and tapestries, this is as happy a museum as you're ever likely to see anywhere in the world.

When Don Quixote came to Barcelona, he watched a naval force set out to do battle with pirates thanks to a signal from the lookout point on Montjuich. This early-warning system by means of flags or bonfires had been operating as early as 1401. But the fortress which stands atop Montjuich today wasn't built until 1640. It was handed over to the city

Work in progress: spires of Gaudi church inspire pride in Catalans

in 1960 and fitted out as the **Museo Militar** (Military Museum).

From the roof of the fortress, you get a sweeping 360-degree panorama of the metropolis of Barcelona and the sea. You can also look straight down onto the port, with its many fascinations.

For visitors with time to spare, Montjuich has more attractions in reserve—a Greek amphitheatre, sports installations, meticulously landscaped terraced gardens, and an amusement park with the full complement of roller-coaster, Ferris wheel and other thrilling rides, plus a special children's amusement park.

The Waterfront *

The boosters of Barcelona always seem to be searching for superlatives. They call this the biggest city on the Mediterranean shore. They also claim that the **Monumento a Colón** (Columbus Monument), between the port and the Rambla, is "the tallest monument to Columbus in the world". Who would dispute this record? The official guidebook says the monument is 193½ feet high. The statue of the explorer is 25 feet tall.

Glass-and-steel commercial castles may come and go, but the **Atarazanas,** or medieval shipyards, are most special. The first work on what became this sprawling building began in the 13th century. This is the only structure of its kind in the world today—an impressive testimony to the level of Catalan industrial architecture in the Middle Ages.

From these royal dockyards were launched the ships which carried the red-and-yellow Catalan flag to the far corners of the world as it was known before Columbus. Since 1941 the **Museo Marítimo** (Maritime Museum) has occupied these appropriate—and roomy—quarters.

The most engrossing display is a full-sized reproduction of the galley *Real*, victorious flagship in the Battle of Lepanto of 1571, where a combined Hispano-Venetian fleet faced the Turks. Elsewhere you can inspect models of fishing boats

---

* The only thing the next items have in common is the geographical coincidence that they are on or near the Barcelona waterfront. They cover a wide swath of the city and a broad range of interests—perhaps something for everybody.

37

and freighters, and glamorous ship figureheads. In the cartography department, look for an atlas drawn in 1439, which once belonged to Amerigo Vespucci.

Across an extremely wide and heavily congested thoroughfare, an unexpected annexe of the Maritime Museum is moored at the wharf of Puerto de la Paz (Port of

Sightseeing tours of Barcelona's busy port include cooling breezes.

Peace). This is a replica of the *Santa María*, Columbus's own flagship—full-sized and said to be authentically fitted out. You may board the floating mini-museum any time during the day.

Like all big ports, this area of Barcelona is strong on at-mosphere. Longshoremen rub shoulders with amateur rod-and-reel-fishermen; guitar-strumming tourists lie back on their knapsacks waiting for the ferryboat to Ibiza. Tugs nudge a huge white cruise liner to a soft berthing. Sightseeing boats, romantically called *gaviotas* (gulls) and *golondrinas* (swallows), stand by to show tourists the harbour from sea-level.

A largely artificial peninsula protecting the port area from the open sea is called **Barceloneta** (Little Barcelona). The residents are something like the local equivalent of Cockneys—certainly "characters" different from the rest. Many of the people here look like stereotyped fishermen, even though they may work in factories or on the wharves. As an 18th-century experiment in urban planning, Barceloneta's street plan is worth a closer look. The blocks are long and uncommonly narrow so that each room of each house faces a street.

Five bus lines terminate at the Paseo Nacional, Barceloneta, site of the city's **Acuario** (Aquarium). Unlike the fishy section of the Barcelona Zoo (see p. 45), this aquarium con-

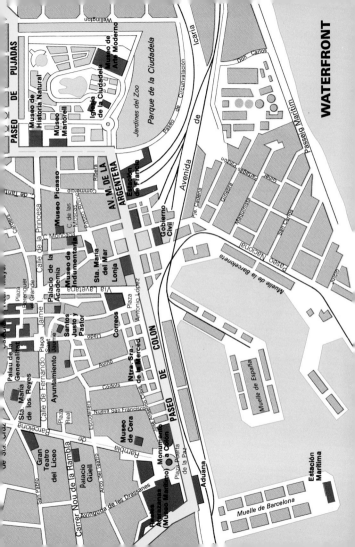

WATERFRONT

cerns itself only with the sea life of the Mediterranean. The lighting is gloomy—for the benefit of the fish, not the people.

Railway yards separate Barceloneta from the Parque de la Ciudadela (see p. 44). The main

On Barcelona waterfront, girls take an ice-cream break in the sun.

terminal, called Estación de Francia because trains from France arrive here, handles only long-distance trains. Commuter trains serving Costa Do-

rada and Costa Brava resorts normally leave from the Cercanías (suburban) terminal, behind the Estación de Francia.

La Lonja (*Llontja* in Catalan) is the Barcelona stock exchange. Since the 14th century, a *bolsa* (exchange) of one sort or another has operated on this spot. Peek through the windows at the seething wheeling and dealing, under timeless Gothic arches.

The cornerstone of the **Iglesia de Santa María del Mar** (Church of St.Mary-of-the-Sea) was laid in 1329. More than any other edifice in Barcelona, this one sums up the real grandeur of 14th-century Catalan churches. The stark beauty of the interior is heightened by the proportions of its soaring arches. The impression of immensity comes, in part, from the uncluttered lines. In addition to its religious functions, Santa María del Mar is often used as a concert hall for programmes of classical music or jazz. It faces the Plaza del Borne, which was Barcelona's main square in the Middle Ages.

Calle de Moncada just beyond would make a worthwhile visit even if it didn't contain one of Barcelona's most popular museums. As early as the 12th century, noble families of Catalonia had begun to build their mansions in this street. You can see their crests carved in stone alongside great portals. Better still, wander into the courtyards of the palaces and relive the glory of those medieval achievements. Take in the detail of the stone-carving on the arches and ceremonial staircases, the ironwork of the railings and lamps, the comforting unity of all the elements.

The **Museo Picasso** is located in two contiguous 13th-century palaces in Calle de Moncada. Though Pablo Ruiz Picasso was born in Málaga, he came to Barcelona at the age of 14 to study art. Those days are documented by drawings and paintings in a style evidently imposed on the young genius by unimaginative teachers. But his true talents, from an even earlier age, are strikingly clear in informal sketches, cartoons and doodles. His large oil painting *Science and Charity,* could have been the work of a master; he was 15 at the time. One large exhibition is devoted to a series of 58 paintings which Picasso donated to the museum in 1968. Of these, 44 are bizarre variations on the theme of *Las Meninas,* the famous Velázquez painting in Madrid's Prado Museum.

Across the street, in another lovely palace, the city of Barcelona has opened the **Museo de Indumentaria** (Costume Museum). Fashions for men, women and children as far back as the 16th century are exhibited according to period and use (military uniforms, bullfighters' costumes or wedding dresses, for instance).

Gaudí and Ensanche

Ensanche means extension or enlargement. In Barcelona, it means the new city which grew beyond the medieval walls in the 19th century. The expansion, several times the area of the existing city, was well planned. Its fine boulevards—the Paseo de Gracia and Rambla de Cataluña, for instance—are expressions of elegance. The very long, wide **Avinguda Diagonal** is not only the main traffic artery from the motorway (expressway) into the city, but an eminently stately avenue with palm trees and interesting architecture. **41**

The Ensanche contains some of the most creative buildings ever designed, the work of Barcelona's inspired *art nouveau* architects at the end of the 19th and beginning of the 20th centuries. The greatest of them all was Antonio Gaudí, a controversial genius born in the Catalonian market town of Reus in 1852. He died in Barcelona in 1926, run down by a tram.

Here are half a dozen typical Gaudí projects you could see in one outing, starting in Old Barcelona and working your way out through the Ensanche:

The **Palacio Güell,** one of several buildings Gaudí designed for his friend and patron, Eusebio Güell, a British-educated Barcelona industrialist, civic leader and nobleman. This palace, just off the bustling Rambla, keeps its biggest innovations out of public view: its front façade, decorated with imaginative ironwork, lacks Gaudí's wit and colour. The rooftop chimney array is so bright and original that it relieves some of the severity.

Casa Batlló. People emerging from the Metro (underground railway) here in Paseo de Gracia may be startled to come face to face with Gaudí's sensuous curves in stone and iron, and his delicate tiles. The house next door, by the brilliant Catalan architect Puig i Cadafalch, conflicts with Gaudí's effort so aggressively that this street is often called the Block of Discord (in Spanish, this involves an ironic play on words).

One of Gaudí's classic buildings: Casa Batlló, in Paseo de Gracia.

42

Casa Milà. On the corner of Paseo de Gracia and Calle de Provenza, this big block of flats stirs strong feelings. Some say it's too heavy, a stone monstrosity; Gaudí fans love its undulating façade, adorned with original wrought-iron-work, and the famous roof-terrace with its weird formations covering chimneys and ventilators.

Casa Vicens. This was designed more than 20 years earlier than Casa Milà, when Gaudí was still groping for his style. In fact, Casa Vicens, a summer home for a rich tile merchant, was Gaudí's first big job as an architect. The distinctive ironwork, the bright ideas with tile may rate admiration, but the overall effect seems incoherent.

Parque Güell. This incomparably inventive park started out as a suburban real estate development which failed. Count Güell and Gaudí wanted to create a perfect garden city for 60 families. But only two houses were sold (Gaudí bought one of them). The happy originality of Güell Park, bought by the city of Barcelona in 1926, delights young and old. See the ginger-bread-type houses, the cheery use of tiles, the serpentine shapes bordering the main plaza. Explore the grounds and discover that the plaza is in fact the roof for what would have been a market-place supported by a thicket of mock-classical columns. The last column in each regiment is playfully askew. Along the woods, walk under the perilously tilted arcade.

Templo Expiatorio de la Sagrada Familia (Holy Family). Gaudí's eternally unfinished "sandcastle cathedral" must be seen; you may not believe it. Wild and wonderful, it is an extravagant hymn to one man's talent and faith. In his first four towers, was Gaudí consciously or unconsciously echoing the filigree of the classic cathedral in the Barrio Gótico? Or the shape of "human castles" of Catalan folklore? If he had lived, would he have continued in the same way? Can one building, however immense, ever successfully combine so many disparate styles? Gaudí's cathedral produces puzzlement and awe. Many Catalans see this stupendous church as an extension of their own faith and strivings; their donations keep the construction work going. **43**

Don't be afraid of the huge cranes hauling pillars and streamlined arches into position. Where else can you stand inside a roofless cathedral and watch it being built? Before your eyes descendants of the great Catalan stonecutters are shaping the faces of angels.

Ciudadela

The residents of Barcelona greatly appreciate El Parque de la Ciudadela (the Park of the Citadel) because it is a big, green refuge from the congestion of the city. They also appreciate it for symbolic reasons going back to the early 18th century.

In those days, the area, called La Ribera, was a pleasant residential suburb of perhaps 10,000 people. Because Barcelona fought on the losing side in the War of the Succession, a vengeful Philip V ordered Ribera levelled. Then he conscripted all the carpenters and masons of Barcelona to build a fortress on the spot.

In the middle of the 19th century, this building of bitter memories was at last demolished. And, characteristically, in its place, the city built a park with gardens, lakes and promenades. Ciudadela Park was the scene of Barcelona's 1888 World Fair.

The great fountain is one of those monumental excesses typical of the period. This titanic mass of sculpture looks like a work of a committee, and indeed it was. One of the contributors was Gaudí, then a student of architecture.

Beloved Barcelona fountain keeps statue of lady dry under umbrella.

The **Museo de Arte Moderno** has a somewhat deceptive title. It is actually devoted to Catalan art of the last 100 years. Outstanding here are the works of Mariano Fortuny (1838–74), a native of Reus, Gaudí's home town near Tarragona. Notice the wealth of astutely recorded detail in *The Vicarage,* and you can't miss *The Battle of Tetuán,* an action-packed panorama which fills a whole wall. Fortuny knew whereof he painted; he was the 19th-century equivalent of a combat photographer in Morocco.

Looking Down

Barcelona is crazy about views from on high.

A modern, modified cable-car built with Swiss technical assistance, floats high above the city between El Paralelo (the Parallel) and Montjuich. An elaborate "aerial rope-way" *(transbordador)* strung from towers 426 feet high serves a similar purpose between the port and Montjuich.

If you have a queasy stomach, try the less daring cog railways running up to Tibidabo or Montjuich.

For a superb panorama of Barcelona, go up to the fortress high on the summit of Montjuich (see p. 37) or to the temple of Tibidabo (p. 46).

Upstairs the museum shows a hotch-potch of modern art, sculpture and *art-nouveau* furnishings. Sharing the floor is the "numismatic cabinet", a seldom-visited museum-within-in-a-museum with 100,000 historic coins.

A sizeable corner of the park is devoted to the **Barcelona Zoo,** an admirable modern version of the conventional

Star of the show at Barcelona zoo: albino gorilla thrives in captivity.

collection of animals. Under a reform programme of the 1950s the zoo eliminated fences, using instead moats or lakes to separate the public from the fauna. Young and old can enjoy six well planned departments: African animals, felines, monkeys, reptiles, birds and fish.

45

Pedralbes

Barcelona's richest residential area, Pedralbes, consists of fashionable blocks of flats, earlier *art nouveau* buildings, and villas discreetly guarded by ornamental fences. (One of those fences, by Gaudí, is a first-class work of art in itself.)

The **Palacio de Pedralbes,** set in a charming park, looks quite livable. Touring its elaborate Italianate salons, you get the feeling that at any moment the keepers might shoo everybody out so that the king could have his lunch. The palace was built in the 1920s as a municipal gift to King Alfonso XIII. Most of the furnishings and works of art were imported from Italy. It is still used as a VIP residence for visiting heads of state, which is why it just might be closed to the public on the day you arrive.

Unless you plan your itinerary very carefully, you might easily miss Pedralbes's other important sight, the **Monasterio de Pedralbes.** The building was begun in 1326. About three dozen nuns live here today.

The cloister, with 25 arches on each side, rises three storeys high. You can meditate (brief-ly) among the poplars and orange trees in the quadrangle. But don't miss the monastery's greatest artistic treasure, in a cramped little chapel lit by two fluorescent tubes. The murals here were painted by Ferrer Bassa, the greatest 14th-century Catalan artist.

Tibidabo

For a first, or last, look at Barcelona no place excels Tibidabo, a mountain about 1,650 feet above the city. On an average of once a month, when visibility is flawless, it's said you can see the mountains of Majorca from here. On an ordinary day you can look down on all Barcelona and a slice of the Costa Dorada as well. Tibidabo can be reached by car, or by an adventurous combination of train, tram and cable car. It's a very popular excursion for the people of Barcelona, especially on a Sunday.

The shrine at the summit is the Templo Expiatorio del Sagrado Corazón (Expiatory Temple of the Sacred Heart of Jesus), a neo-Gothic extravaganza erected in 1911. A huge statue of a Christ with outstretched arms stands upon the topmost tower.

Just beneath the church is a big amusement park with a roller coaster, an old-fashioned aeroplane-go-round, and other rides for children or light-hearted adults. There are also hotels on Tibidabo, as well as restaurants, snack-bars, sports facilities, an observatory and a TV tower.

Nothing shy about the pigeons in Plaza de Cataluña at lunch time.

Sitges and the Coast South of Barcelona

The coastal landscape on the south side of Barcelona has its share of cliffs and coves, but consists mainly of broad sand beaches. For variety there are appealing fishing villages, and even a stretch of green paddy fields. Along with the scenery

near outskirts hold practically no interest for tourists. (A vital exception is the international airport, close by the sea at Prat de Llobregat.)

The first resort town following Prat, CASTELLDEFELS, enjoys an extremely long sand beach. Low-rise hotels, apartment houses and villas exploit the coastline, while the town centre looks inland. In the 13th

and water sports the region is rich in history and culture.

Leaving Barcelona towards the south-west the suburbs can't seem to decide whether they are agricultural or factory towns—or just half-hearted resorts. Whatever the label, the

century, when Castelldefels first entered the history books, the sea was a danger. Watch-towers, some still standing, guarded against pirates. The castle which gave the town its name, impressive enough from afar, has become dilapidated since its last renovation in 1897.

A small **museum** is maintained in a recently restored mansion below the castle. The exhibits in the Casa de Cultura include prehistoric tools and 19th-century farm implements.

Beyond Castelldefels the railway line cuts through mountains, while the road winds around them the hard way, often skirting cliffsides dramatically. Two villages appear at unexpected inlets. GARRAF, an industrial town, has a marina and unobtrusive villas. VALLCARCA, with its own cargo port, is not a tourist town at all.

By the time the coastline begins to level out, the scene changes dramatically. **Sitges,** an internationally admired resort, combines natural beauty, liveliness and dignity.

Sitges is one of the rare Spanish coastal resorts which has maintained its identity, avoiding the monstrosities of tourist architecture while still encouraging tourism. This is one town without repetitive high-rise hotels. The swinging "downtown" area lives one life; further along the seafront promenade, the "other half"—largely wealthy families from Barcelona—enjoys a quieter

existence in villas hidden behind high, trimmed hedges. The beach is nearly three miles long—enough for crowd-lovers and seekers of serenity as well. Bathing is safe for children, as it tends to be all the way from here to Tarragona and beyond.

The parish church, on a promontory, was built between the 16th and 18th centuries,

Surfboard plus sail equals exciting sport, only for the well-balanced.

but sacked during the Civil War. It may not be an architectural gem, but its dramatic setting makes up for that; at night, it is skilfully illuminated **49** against the sky. Just behind the church, two museums contribute to the cultural atmosphere which helps explain the town's long-standing appeal to artists and intellectuals. The **Museo Cau Ferrat** (Cau Ferrat—or "iron lair"—Museum) contains a moving El Greco portrait, *The Tears of St. Peter*, as well as a blazingly colourful early oil by Picasso, *Corrida*

After an exhausting day of tanning, tourists stroll beneath the palms of Sitges and plan the night's agenda.

de toros. Here you can also see many works by Santiago Rusiñol (1861–1931), the Catalan artist and writer who gave the building to the town. Next-door, the **Museo Mar i Cel del Mar** (Mar i Cel Museum), in a 14th-century palace, displays medieval sculpture and religious paintings. A few streets inland, another museum is aimed at people who don't normally go to museums, least of all at a resort. The **Museo Romántico** (Romantic Museum) of Sitges is an old aristocratic home lavishly decorated in 19th-century style and full of the fascinating *things* of the era—furniture, clocks and music boxes that work.

With its whitewashed houses facing narrow hilly streets, its gourmet restaurants, pizza parlours and flamenco nightclubs, and its mild climate, Sitges attracts holiday-makers over many months of the year. A very special time, however, comes every spring. At the fiesta of Corpus Christi the streets are covered with fresh flowers—a quarter of a million of them, in inventive patterns. The beauty couldn't be more fleeting, for the flower carpets last just one day.

A few miles down the coast

the city of VILLANUEVA Y GELTRÚ has an extensive sand beach but much less tourist development than Sitges.

Befitting a town of about 45,000 people, there is a serious museum—the **Museo Balaguer**—devoted mainly to 19th-century paintings by Catalan artists.

Villanueva y Geltrú also has its non-serious museum, a first cousin of the Romantic Museum in Sitges. **Casa Papiol,** an 18th-century mansion, recreates a vanished way of life—right down to the stables and wine-cellar, and a trim garden in which graceful swans reside alongside magnificent peacocks.

The only excitements between the villages of CUBELLAS and CUNIT are the River Foix and the boundary line dividing the provinces of Barcelona and Tarragona.

Slightly further down the coast, CALAFELL is much more of a tourist centre. With its two-mile long beach, gently slanting into a calm sea, Calafell was a natural choice for exploitation.

COMARRUGA, with nearly three miles of sand beach, has been transformed into a fashionable holiday resort with big hotels to supplement its comfortable villas. It's a spa and sporting centre as well. Only a few years ago, Comarruga was no more than an obscure appendage of the inland rail junction of San Vicente de Calders.

The coast road along here—usually jammed in summer—follows the Roman highway to Tarragona. A startling reminder of this confronts motorists not far beyond Comarruga. In the middle of the road stands a triumphal arch—not one of those ugly neo-classical models commemorating some recent war, but the real thing. This well-proportioned monument, tall as a three-floor building has been there since the 2nd century A.D. The **Arco de Bará** (Arch of Bará), as it's called, now stands in a position of honour in a small island of green; instead of going under the arch, as it did for hundreds of years, the road now makes a detour around it.

TORREDEMBARRA, the next big resort centre, is expanding along its wide sand beach with new hotels, villas and flats. The local castle, until recently in private hands, is being restored by the government.

The next castle down the **51**

road, in the inland town of ALTAFULLA, is said to have been begun in the 11th century. Altafulla is the kind of village where the children wave at foreigners. Its medieval back streets are as quiet as a museum.

TAMARIT Castle, visible from afar, juts out above the sea. Even though holiday-makers swim from beaches on either side of Tamarit, the castle looks thoroughly invulnerable. It may have been built in the 11th century, but has been considerably restored since then.

Finally, three notable historical sites as the traveller approaches the Tarragona area.

El Medol, a Roman stone-quarry, is right along the motor-way *(autopista)* at the last service area before Tarragona. This man-made crater provided some of the stone for the Roman developments in Tarragona. You can almost see the same grain in the rock as in the great blocks of the city wall.

Right at the edge of the old coast road (N. 340), the so-called **Torre de los Escipiones** (Tower of the Scipios) was a Roman funeral monument.

Little can be said with assurance about this structure, probably a 1st century A.D. tomb. The sculpted figures of two men in Roman military dress can still be distinguished, but time has erased most other details.

The considerate highway engineers provided parking space and sightseeing facilities in honour of another ancient

Seaside apparition near Tarragona: austere, daunting Tamarit Castle.

structure along the route, known locally as **El Puente del Diablo** (Devil's Bridge). This perfect Roman aqueduct, a double-decker of stone, carried Tarragona's water supply from the River Gayá. No viaduct of today is more sound or practical—or more graceful.

Tarragona

Pop. 100,000
(Barcelona, 98 km.)

In the 3rd century B.C., the Romans landed at Tarragona and set up military and political headquarters. They liked its strategic location, mild climate and wine. So will you.

Tarraco, as the town was called, became the capital of tour of Tarragona. The middle of this elongated oblong plaza is now a municipal car park. The city hall occupies one end. But Plaça de la Font is built on the site of the Roman Circus, the 2nd or 3rd century A.D. precursor of a bullring.

Just behind the city hall, a modern avenue called Vía de l'Imperi skilfully recreates the grace of Roman times. The

Rome's biggest Spanish province. It grew to a population of 30,000 and coined its own money. It was one of the formidable imperial capitals of Antiquity. So much was built, and so much remains, that Tarragona sometimes feels like a time machine. Turn a corner and you flip from the 20th century to the 15th, or the 1st.

For example: **Plaça de la Font,** an apparently unexceptional spot to begin a walking

Romans constructed amphitheatre overlooking the sea in Tarragona.

mosaics are reminiscent of the walks of Pompeii. The Roman column is authentic. This short street climbs to one of Tarragona's outstanding features: the **Passeig Arqueològic** (archaeological promenade), a close-up tour of the ancient city wall.

Nothing here is more than **53**

about 2,100 years old—even the foundation of the wall, composed of titanic uncut stones weighing up to 35 tons each. They are often referred to as "cyclopean" because of their enormity and irregular shape.

Not only is the wall, with its towers and gateways, a notable historical and architectural attraction, there are also fine panoramas of the countryside and the sea. But don't be misled when you discover, just down the hill, a well preserved open-air Greek theatre. It's a municipal auditorium, built in 1970.

The Passeig Arqueològic, among other impressive ancient sites in Tarragona, is revealed in all its glory on summer nights, when it's bathed in illumination.

Leaving the last gateway, we follow the Passeig Torroja outside the wall as it curves toward the sea. A small park surrounding the Creu de Sant Antoni (St. Anthony's Cross) erected in 1604 faces one of the main gates of the walled city. The Portal de Sant Antoni (St. Anthony's Gateway) leads into the labyrinth of medieval Tarragona, a markedly Mediterranean city with flowerpots in the windows, laundry hang-

ing out to dry and canaries in cages on the walls.

If you can resist wandering at random through this splash of local colour, stick to the Vía Granada until you reach the Plaça del Rei (King's Square). The **Museu Arqueològic** here is a modern, well designed exhibit of delicate mosaics, ancient utensils, pre-Roman, Roman and Spanish coins.

Adjoining the museum, the building once known as the King's Castle is now called the **Pretori Romà** (Roman Pretorium). This much-restored 2,000-year-old fortress contains more archaeological items, including a beautifully sculpted marble sarcophagus found in the sea. You can follow underground passages which linked the castle with the circus (now Plaça de la Font). The vaults served as dungeons in Antiquity, and again during the Spanish Civil War.

Walking from here toward the sea, you can look down upon the Roman **amphitheatre** built into the hillside. During excavations in 1953, an early Christian church was found on the site of the amphitheatre. Presumably, the primitive basilica was a memorial to a bish-

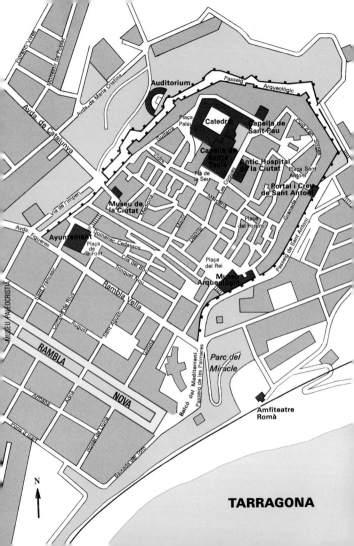

op and two deacons burned to death there in A.D. 259.

Here, above the ruins and the sea, begins what's called the **Balcó del Maditerrani** (Balcony of the Mediterranean), a cliffside promenade, Tarragona's pride. The view of the sea is unbeatable.

Tarragona's **Rambla** runs uphill and ends at the Balcony of the Mediterranean. Otherwise, it's reminiscent of Barcelona's famous promenade, with many trees, outdoor cafés and a great variety of shops all along it. The statue at the top end of the Rambla honours Admiral Roger de Lauria, a swashbuckling 13th-century hero of the Kingdom of Catalonia and Aragon.

Two other important ancient sites—beyond the area of the walking tour—must be mentioned before we turn to medieval Tarragona.

Near the central market and post office, with its entrance in Carrer Lleida, the remains of the **Roman Forum** have been unearthed. Unlike most archaeological excavations, this one is *above* the level of the present-day city, so two halves of the forum are now connected by a footbridge above Carrer Soler. You can wander around the area at will, visualizing the layout of houses, shops and other amenities. This well-kept open-air museum is completely hemmed in by a modern city, yet keeps a stately calm.

On the edge of the city, overlooking the River Francolí, an extraordinary museum has been established in an unlikely place. The **Necròpoli i Museu**

Paleocristià (Necropolis and Paleo-Christian Museum), a cemetery for Tarragona's early Christians, is about as big as three football fields. The site has been left essentially as it was. You can walk along the observation platforms looking down upon hundreds of graves, urns and even bones lying where they were uncovered. And in the adjoining museum you can see the best of the finds. Several 5th-century sarcophagi are sculpted with astounding skill.

Medieval Tarragona

Walking up Carrer Sant Agustí from the Rambla, the old city soon closes in. By the time the street's name has changed—to Major—you can feel the throb of real main-stream Mediterranean life. The road turns a bend and suddenly the **Cathedral** comes into view, strangely cropped at the edges by its elevation and the narrowness of the street.

A flight of 19 steps leads from the end of Carrer Major to the Plà de la Seu, an attractive, almost intimate square before the church. But don't overlook the last cross-

street before the cathedral— the Mercería (Haberdashery Street) with its medieval porticoes. A shop here advertises canaries; a female costs half the price of a male (presumably because females can't sing).

Ancient tomb sculpture (opposite) *is one facet of Tarragona beauty. Streets, cathedral add to mood.*

Surrounding walls and tricks of perspective may distort your estimation of the cathedral's size. The area of the façade is deceptive. But the great Gothic doorway, and one of Europe's largest rose windows above it, provide a clue.

Follow the arrows to the tourist entrance, far around the church to the left, via the cloister. Construction of this cathedral, on the site of a Roman temple to Jupiter, was begun in 1171, and it was consecrated in 1331. The architectural styles inside the cathedral mix Romanesque and Gothic; the overall effect, looking up at the great vaulted ceiling, is austere majesty.

The **main altarpiece,** carved in alabaster by the 15th-century Catalan master Pere Johan, shows splendid lifelike detail. It is dedicated to St. Thecla, the local patron saint. She is said to have been converted to Christianity by St. Paul, who, according to legend, preached in Tarragona.

To the right of the high altar is the tomb of Prince Don Juan de Aragón, an archbishop of Tarragona who died in 1334 at the age of 33. Note the sensitive carving on the sepulchre. **58** The artist's identity is unknown; the influence seems to be Italian.

Nineteen chapels fill the sides of the church. Their design and decoration tend to extremes—either unforgettably beautiful, or unexpectedly 19th-century kitsch. Don't miss **three chapels:** Capella de Nostra Senyora de Montserrat (Chapel of Our Lady of Montserrat), with its 15th-century altarpiece; the filigreed sculpture in the 14th-century Capella de Santa Maria dels Sastres (Chapel of St. Mary of the Tailors) and the 18th-century Capella de Santa Tecla (Chapel of St. Thecla).

And if the art appreciation and sheer foot-slogging become a bit too much, just take a seat in the congregation and look up at the sunbeams piercing the filters of the rose window.

Outside, again, the **cloister** offers some surprises. First, its size—some 150 feet down each side. The quadrangle is so big that there is little shade, and perhaps less feeling of serenity than in other cloisters of the 12th and 13th centuries. But notice the sculptural innovations and details. Everyone stops to figure out the relief known as the Procession of the

Rats, a wry fable carved 700 years before the invention of Mickey Mouse. Built into one of the walls is another unexpected feature—a Moslem monument of marble. The date on its inscription works out to A.D. 960. This *mihrab* or shrine is believed to have arrived in Tarragona as a battle trophy.

The cathedral's **Museu Dio-**

Fishermen back from sea assign repair of nets to their womenfolk.

cesà (Diocesan Museum) possesses prehistoric and Roman archaeological relics, medieval religious paintings, and a large and valuable collection of tapestries.

Tarragona-on-Sea

For a drastic change of pace, take a bus or taxi, or a very long walk, down to the Tarragona waterfront district unaccountably known as **El Serrall** (the harem). This is clearly an important fishing centre, a radical escalation from the usual quaint port found elsewhere along this coast. In the afternoon the big trawlers come back from the open sea. Trays of ice and big refrigerated lorries are waiting on the quayside. Before disembarking, the tanned fishermen clean and separate the different species of fish in the hold. They swallow the last trickle of wine from the ship's *porrón*, then step ashore to bargain with wholesalers over prices. Elsewhere along the quay, half a dozen women seated under parasols mend the huge fishnets bound for sea before the next dawn.

For local colour, and aroma, El Serrall is hard to match. If you have half a chance, eat in one of the nearby fish restaurants. Tarragona cooking is known far and wide in Catalonia, and the ingredients couldn't be fresher. **59**

South-West of Tarragona

While Tarragona has its own municipal beaches, the nearest resort of international renown is **Salou,** about 10 kilometres down the coast. This cosmopolitan centre calls itself Playa de Europa (beach of Europe). Salou's good fortune is due to its two-mile-long beach, bor-

The town of Salou (pronounced Sal-OH-oo) distinguishes itself with almost universal good taste: the villas and blocks of flats maintain high architectural standards, the gardens are well kept and even the modern monument to James I the Conqueror fits right into place. The beach at Salou was the port of embarcation for James' armada which

dered by a lavish promenade with solid rows of stubby palm trees and masses of colourfully arranged flowers. What's more, swimmers who need more adventure can desert the beach and opt for half-hidden coves around rugged Cape Salou.

Real life along the coast: fishermen crouch over nets, while shoppers exchange strong opinions.

wrested Majorca from the Moors in 1229.

Salou's suburb of VILAFORTUNY, with another long beach, consists primarily of exclusive villas protected by high fences or hedges. The landscaping is exceptional.

CAMBRILS, often described as a "typical seafaring village", is a standard fishing port which happens to interrupt the solid line of beaches down the coast. Its charm centres on the large fleet of *bous*—small fishing boats carrying over-sized lamps for night duty. Cambrils can claim to be something of a gourmet town. Its waterfront counts more fine seafood restaurants than many a metropolis. Enthusiasts drive there from miles around, not for the water sports nor the scenery, but just for a meal.

MIAMI PLAYA has plenty of sand and sea, yet doesn't quite live up to the glamour of its name. It's just a quiet resort community of villas and apartments and family hotels. But the setting is dramatic—hills and cliffs push right onto the beaches.

The small resort of HOSPITALET DEL INFANTE (Hospice of the Prince) is built alongside the ruins of a 14th-century

hospice for pilgrims, after which the town was named.

Between Hospitalet and the next coastal resort, Ametlla de Mar, the shore is almost undeveloped, with one startling exception. The nuclear power station of Vandellós looms up like a science-fiction spaceport. At any rate, the titanic red and white main building looks as if it would be more com-

fortable at Cape Canaveral than on this beachfront. Power lines fan out into the countryside.

AMETLLA, by happy contrast, is a no-nonsense, picture-postcard fishing village. Four nearby beaches make it some- **61** thing of a tourist centre, but this hasn't marred the town's picturesque charm. With its solid sea-wall, Fishermen's Guild, ice factory and a few cafés, it remains a genuine fishing port.

Just past the small port of AMPOLLA, the remarkable **Ebro Delta** begins. This lush, tropical peninsula—more than 100 square miles—was created from the mud travelling down the River Ebro all the way from Zaragoza. The river continues its land reclamation work and the delta expands quite perceptibly each year. A rich rice-growing district, it's all so flat that sometimes, with the reeds growing tall along the back roads, the level of the canals seems higher than the road. The delta is a rallying point for migratory birds—and for bird-watchers with binoculars, cameras, or guns.

AMPOSTA, a town of nearly 15,000 people, dominates the delta. It is considered a key centre for sports fishing. In earlier times, Amposta guarded the river route and charged a toll on ships heading inland.

TORTOSA (population 50,000) commands both banks of the Ebro, which explains its strategic importance since ancient times. Julius Caesar awarded Tortosa the title of independent municipality. The elaborate fortress at the top of the town belonged to the Moors, who held out there at length during the Christian Reconquest in 1148. The castle of San Juan is still known by its Arabic name, La Zuda.

Tortosa's **cathedral,** now a national monument, appears at first sight to be abandoned and menaced by the town around it. But you can enter through the cloister, which is well shaded by tall pines. The cathedral, built during the 14th, 15th and 16th centuries, is a classic example of Catalan Gothic. Don't miss the 14th-century triptych, painted on wood, and the two 15th-century carved stone pulpits.

Attempts to make the River Ebro a major navigational channel—Aragon's age-old dream of an outlet to the sea—have been dormant for 50 years. But the river still permeates everyday life in Tortosa. It looks as if it's carrying all the soil of Spain out to the Mediterranean—not the sort of river you'd want to swim in.

The last town of any note along the coast, before the provincial boundary marks the

end of the Costa Dorada and the beginning of the Costa del Azahar, is SAN CARLOS DE LA RÁPITA. Its huge natural harbour, supplemented by man-made sea-walls, serves a prosperous fishing fleet. A good deal of ship-building activity may be seen here, as well. But what makes San Carlos (population about 10,000) different from all the other towns is its **main square.**

This gigantic plaza looks just the place for a coronation parade. It is so enormous, and the town itself so small, that there aren't enough shops and offices to fill its perimeter; many of the buildings are just private houses. The square was a city-planning brainstorm of Charles III, an eccentric 18th-century ruler who pictured San Carlos as a port of international significance. The grandiose project died with him in 1788, but the legacy of his street plan and the melancholy square remain. Impertinently, the main road to Valencia goes right down the middle of Charles's freakish plaza.

Traditional fishing fleet occupies waterfront in Cambrils but tourists coexist and exploit nearby beaches.

Inland Excursions

✦ Montserrat
(Barcelona, 62 km.)

For 700 years, pilgrims have been climbing the mighty rock formations to the monastery of Montserrat. Now that donkeys have been replaced by cable cars and excursion coaches, about a million people make the trip every year. The statistics don't say how many are pilgrims and how many are just sightseers, but one way or the other, visitors feel uplifted in this mountain redoubt.

Geographically and spiritually, Montserrat is the heart of Catalonia. The ancient Benedictine monastery, tucked into the rock, houses the patron of the Catalans—a 12th-century polychrome wood image of the Virgin Mary called **La Moreneta,** the little brown Madonna. Notice her nose: long, thin and pointed; it's the same nose you'll see on half the faces in the congregation. It's a thoroughly Catalan nose.

The brown madonna is so avidly venerated here that you may have to queue for 15 minutes for a look. The statue, in a niche above the basilica's high altar, is protected by glass. But a circle cut out of the shield permits the faithful to touch or kiss the image's outstretched right hand. Your visit may be delayed a minute or two while formally dressed newly-weds are ushered to the head of the line to pray and be photographed alongside La Moreneta (an unusual number of weddings take place in the pompous basilica, often witnessed by thousands of foreign tourists).

Tour companies run half-day and full-day excursions to Montserrat from Barcelona and all the major resorts of the Costa Dorada.

A highlight of any visit to Montserrat is its choir. The young choristers of the Escolanía, thought to be the oldest music-school in Europe, perform in the monastery at midday. The angelic voices sing as inspiringly as advertised.

A guided tour of the monastery concentrates on its **museum,** devoted to works of art and history. Several rooms cover "the Biblical East" through relics thousands of years old from Mesopotamia, Egypt and Palestine. Gold and silver chalices and reliquaries are on view. And the museum's art gallery owns a number of notable paintings, including a striking *Portrait of St. Jerome* by Caravaggio.

The monks here are rarely in view, busy as they are elsewhere with prayer, meditation, study in a 200,000-volume library, and down-to-earth labour. They make pottery, run a goldsmith's workshop and a printing plant, and distill a pleasant herbal liqueur called *Aromas de Montserrat.*

For a few pesetas, you can sample *Aromas* in the monastery's tourist bar, which also dispenses coffee and soft and hard drinks. It is one of a disconcertingly mundane array of shops and services for visitors. Montserrat has a hotel, a hairdressing salon, self-service restaurant and a souvenir supermarket.

The brisk commercial atmosphere disillusions some pilgrims, but the overall effect of Montserrat and its eerie mountains remains powerful.

In the basilica, with its eighton stone altar made of the mountain itself, sit and listen to the boys sing the *Virolai,* Montserrat's hymn. Perhaps you'll be able to distinguish some of the words—*Montserrat* and *la catalana terra.* The Catalan land and Montserrat have been inseparable

Symbol of Catalanism, Montserrat monastery is tucked into the rock.

for centuries. You'll begin to understand how when you hear the congregation join the choir in this anthem. **65**

Poblet
(Barcelona, 132 km.)

When you've seen one monastery, you have definitely not seen them all. The medieval fortress-monastery of Poblet contrasts sharply with Montserrat. Few tourists crowd Poblet, 45 kilometres northwest of Tarragona. While Montserrat clings to its granite

This powerful Cistercian monastery was founded more than 800 years ago by the count of Barcelona, Ramón Berenguer IV, as a gesture of thanksgiving for the reconquest of Catalonia from the Moors. The royal connections brought the monastery fame, fortune and historical importance. Poblet's church, as large as a cathedral, contains the **tombs** of the kings

mountain, Poblet sprawls upon a wide-open plateau amidst fertile hillsides. Montserrat's buildings, almost totally destroyed in 1811, were replaced by undistinguished architecture. Poblet's buildings were plundered and pillaged in 1835, but lovingly restored—and they have great architectural importance, as well as beauty.

of Aragon, suspended on unique low arches in the cross vault. Here lie James I the Conqueror (Jaime I el Conquistador), Peter the Ceremonious (Pedro el Ceremonioso), John I (Juan I) and his two wives, and Alphonse the Chaste (Alfonso el Casto). (Only fragments of the original sculpture were preserved, so the pantheon of today is a skilled reproduction.) Another outstanding example of alabaster sculpture is the **altarpiece** by the 16th-century artist Damia Forment. Tourists are guided through the most historic halls making up the monastic community.

The real appreciation of a monastic mood comes in the **cloister,** with its rose bushes

Beauty and tranquillity in medieval surroundings at Poblet monastery.

and four brooding poplars, the quiet relieved only by the trickling fountain and the twitter of birds. Beauty and serenity reign in this historic quadrangle.

Santes Creus

(Barcelona, 98 km.)

About 40 kilometres from Poblet—the route goes through the district market town of Valls (see p. 68)—another great monastery sprawls among the vineyards. The Cistercian monastery of Santes Creus was founded in the middle of the 12th century. While Poblet is a working monastery, Santes Creus has been preserved as a museum. Thus all buildings are on view here—from the dormitories to the kitchen.

The **cloister,** a pioneering work of Catalan Gothic design, dates from the beginning of the 14th century. Notice the stone carvings on the arches and in unexpected places on the walls: heraldic designs, animals, sometimes humorous faces.

The **church,** begun in 1174, is austere and powerful. The kings of Aragon and Catalonia were patrons of Santes Creus; the monastery's abbot was royal chaplain. And here, opposite the presbytery, are royal sepulchres. King Peter III the Great (Pedro el Grande) is buried here in a temple-within-in-a-church—a tall Gothic tabernacle. The royal remains **67**

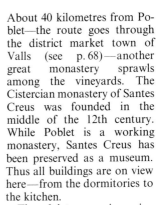

were interred in a Roman bath resting on four stone lions and covered by an elaborate alabaster tombstone.

In addition to several tombs of lesser grandeur, the monastery reveals its regal connections in the so-called "Royal Palace"—living quarters surrounding a perfect 14th-century patio of delicate arches and a finely sculpted staircase.

David Baird

Human castle team assembles itself gingerly at breakneck speed.

Valls
(Barcelona, 105 km.)

The busy provincial town of Valls (population about 15,000) is famous throughout Catalonia for two odd superlatives. It produces the highest-rising human castles and the most delicious onions.

The *castellers* (see FOLKLORE, page 71) of Valls—known here as the *Xiquets* (pronounced SHEE-kets)—are looked up to both figuratively and literally. No other team in Catalonia has ever managed such skyscrapers of boys balanced atop men astride giants.

As for the onions—called *calçots*—they are gently cooked when very young, dipped in a special sauce, and consumed with grilled sausage or lamb. Summer tourists miss the boat, for this feast only takes place from about December to April.

The next best treat for visitors is *Firagost,* as the festivities of the first half of August are called. Farmers from the entire district bring their finest flowers and fruits to Valls for a tribute to the bounty of the earth. It's a lively time, with folk-dancing, fireworks and, of course, personal appearances by the *Xiquets.*

Vilafranca del Penedés
(Barcelona, 54 km.)

In the year 1217 the Catalonian parliament—the Cortes Catalanes—convened for the first time. The place: Vilafranca del Penedés, on a fertile plateau midway between Barcelona and Tarragona. Since then the population has grown tenfold, to 20,000. But the city still commands more fame than its size would justify. Thousands of tourists who come here by car or coach think of Vilafranca as Wine City. This is the home of Spain's most impressive **wine museum.**

You don't have to be a connoisseur, or even a drinker, to find fascination in the exhibits. Lively three-dimensional dioramas illustrate the business and pleasure of wine through the ages. You can see the actual wine presses which were crushing the grapes 2,000 years ago. And one hall displays glasses, bottles and jugs covering centuries of thirst. There is even an art gallery devoted to the vine and its ramifications.

The wine museum shares its quarters with the **Museo Municipal** (city museum) of Vilafranca, devoted primarily to geological exhibits and prehistoric finds. The building used to be a palace of the counts of Barcelona and the kings of Aragon.

Vilafranca del Penedés—often seen in its Castilian form Villafranca del Panadés—has one other enthusiasm. The local team of *castellers*—human pyramids—so captivates the citizens that in 1963 a monument was unveiled in their honour. It's right there in Plaza Jaime I, an interpretation of a five-story *pilar*; locally it's claimed to be among the world's tallest modern statues.

Several wine producers in the Penedés district invite tourists to visit their premises for an explanation of the production process and a sample of the end result. An impressive establishment at San Sadurní de Noya, the Codorniú caves, attracts many excursion coaches. From January to June, this one plant turns out thousands of bottles of "sparkling cellar wine" per day.

Andorra
(Barcelona, 220 km.)

Excursion firms all along the Costa Dorada advertise gruelling one-day trips to Andorra, **69** the 188-square-mile principality huddling between mountain peaks in the Pyrenees. With well over 200 kilometres of travel in each direction, not much time is left for sightseeing in tiny Andorra itself. In fact, most of the visit is devoted to shopping. Since Andorra is free of the taxes which afflict neighbouring countries, the price of almost

are almost universally understood, while English and German are most useful in the shops.

Aside from the crass business of bargain-hunting, take time for a stroll through ANDORRA LA VELLA, the capital. Most of the principality's permanent residents live there. Visit the Casa de la Vall, a 16th-century building in which

everything comes as a refreshing surprise. After 700 years of fiercely defended independence, the country's spectacular scenery now takes second place; most of today's visitors are heading straight for the bulging shops of Calle Merrinitx.

Andorra is the only country in which the official language is Catalan. Spanish and French

Flag and escutcheon proclaim individuality of state of Andorra, protected by peaks of Pyrenees.

the country's parliament and court are housed. The nation's archives rest in a chest secured with six locks, the keys to which are held in the six parishes.

What to Do

Folklore

The stately *sardana,* the national dance of Catalonia, evokes an uncommon affection and interest among the people. The music may grate at first, because of its hints of Arabic woodwinds and the trills of Italian operetta. It also endures longer than one would have thought possible: just four lines of music repeated without mercy for up to ten minutes. This is a rugged workout for the dancers, who link hands, young and old together, friends or strangers, in an ancient type of round dance. Serious *sardana* dancers change into traditional light shoes—*alpargatas*—but anyone can join in. The musical instruments accompanying these floating but subtle exertions are a sort of oboe and a small flute and a small drum, the latter two played in tandem, one for each hand.

A dance for specialists is the *Ball dels Bastons* (dance of the sticks) which enlivens many fiestas. Highly trained young men or boys in costume perform an intricate and potentially somewhat dangerous stick-dance, reminiscent of fencing and jousting.

Castellers are the men and boys who climb upon each other's shoulders to form human towers. The sport requires the skill of the mountain climber and the tightrope walker, plus trust and teamwork to the extreme. One false move could tumble the whole pyramid.

The *castellers* will always climb barefoot. The unsung, unseen heroes are the behemoths on the bottom layer. The most pampered participant is the local boy—perhaps only six years old—who has been trained to scamper to the summit like a monkey. When he reaches the top of the pyramid, the *enxaneta* (weathercock) releases one hand for a couple of seconds to wave a victory sign. The crowd cheers. Deftly, the castle comes apart from the top down.

During religious processions and other combinations of solemnity and fireworks, many towns parade their giant effigies *(Gegants* and *Cabezudos).* Skilled crews hidden beneath these figures, which are three times human size, balance the heavy statues and even make them dance. At some festivals, firecracker squads reminiscent of Chinese dragon impersona-

Earnest musicians set the pace for sardana *dancing in Barcelona.*

tors plough through the crowds, generating blinding glare and deafening noise. No one finds it incongruous when all this is followed by a plodding procession of little girls and old women holding lighted tapers and religious banners. The quick-changing moods are contagious.

The Bullfight

Nothing is more uniquely Spanish—or incomprehensible to the foreigner—than the *fiesta brava,* the bullfight. If you've never experienced this spectacle, you may want to seize the chance on your visit to the Coṣta Dorada. Although bullfighting is not a particularly Catalonian pursuit it is extremely popular, particularly in Barcelona, which has two bullrings.

Understand from the beginning that the bullfight is not regarded as a sport. A sport is a contest between equals; in bullfighting the odds are weighted heavily against the bull. The *corrida* is a ritualistic preparation for the bull's death. Yet, every time the *torero* enters the ring, he knows his own life is in danger. (Call him a *torero,* please, and not *toreador,* which you may have picked up—erroneously—from Bizet's *Carmen.)* In the first *tercio* (third) of the fight, the matador meets the fierce bull, takes his measure and begins to tire him using the big red and yellow *capote.*

In the second *tercio* the *picador,* a mounted spearman in Sancho Panza costume, lances the bull's shoulder muscles, and the deft *banderilleros* stab darts into the animal's shoulders.

Finally, the matador returns to taunt the bull with the small, dark-red *muleta* cape, eventually dominating the beast. Finally, as the bull awaits the death he must now sense is inevitable, the *torero* lunges for the kill.

Flamenco

Spain's best-known entertainment, after the bullfight, is flamenco—throbbing guitars, stamping heels and songs that gush from the soul. Many of the songs resemble the wailing chants of Arab music, which may be a strong clue to flamenco's origins. Throughout the Costa Dorada flamenco shows

The bull staggers to its knees, bringing the corrida to an end.

You may be upset or fascinated or simply confused by an afternoon at the *plaza de toros*. But you will have witnessed a violent act which at times contains touching beauty. With luck, you'll come to understand why this ballet of death is considered an art form in Spain.

are popular tourist attractions.

There are two main groups of songs: one, bouncier and more cheerful, is known as the *cante chico* (a light tune). The second group of songs, called *cante jondo,* deals with love, death, all the human drama, in the slow, piercing style of the great flamenco singers.

But it's the *cante chico* you'll hear at the nightclub floorshow called the *tablao flamenco*. Less dramatic and soulsearching, the *cante chico* is **73** basically lighthearted but can be philosophical and touching. It all makes for a big night out with excitement and colour. And perhaps you'll come away with a feeling for the real flamenco: an ageless beauty in a dramatic ruffle dress, clapping hands as fast as a hummingbird flaps its wings, defying an arrogant dark man chanting with his eyes half-closed.

Shopping

Shopping Hours

Along the coast most shops are open from about 9 a.m. to 1 p.m. and again from 4 to 8 p.m.

A significant exception: the big, non-stop department stores of Barcelona, which disregard the siesta tradition.

(Bars and cafés normally remain open from around 8 a.m. until midnight or later, with no afternoon break.)

Best Buys

Catalonian ceramics can be primitive or sophisticated, but they're usually quite original. Note the cheerful colours on the sleek modern bowls, which resemble Scandinavian dishware, and the subtle innovations in traditional pots and vases. Decorative tiles can be artistic or just witty with slogans in the Catalan language.

An intensive cottage industry along the coast produces leatherwork, mainly handbags and items of clothing. The quality of the leather and the workmanship is erratic and so is the style, but good buys can be found if you can spare the time to search for them.

Shoes often cost less in Spain than elsewhere in Europe but the workmanship of cheap models is unimpressive. Stylish shoes and boots can be top-class but expensive.

Embroidery, lacework and woven goods such as rugs and bedspreads are produced in coastal villages which keep alive the old patterns and skills. Notice the women of the knitting circles hiding from the hot sun; their products are often on sale in the local shops.

Jewellery, either simple modern designs or traditional styles with lots of silver or gold filigree, can include bargains for the knowledgeable.

For less expansive budgets, there are records of Catalan music—the *sardana* played by those reed bands, or emotional choral works—to remind you always of your holiday.

Or local glasswork, such as the *porróns,* from which wine is projected through the air to the consumer—or which just look intriguing on a shelf.

Or wooden candlesticks in locally carved designs.

Or vaguely snobbish miniature reproductions of Leonardo da Vinci inventions.

Among "best buys" of any trip to Spain are alcohol and tobacco. These are so cheap, by other European and American standards, that there's no need for duty-free shops. Many famous foreign drinks are bottled in Catalonia under licence, and cost the consumer a fraction of the price at home. But for a souvenir gift, buy a bottle of one of the regional liqueurs.

Souvenirs

If you insist on buying "traditional" Spanish souvenirs, there's no shortage of shops overflowing with mock bullfighter swords from Toledo, inlaid Moorish-style chess sets, imitation antique pistols, bullfight posters (with or without your own name imprinted as a star matador), statuettes of Don Quixote, and the typical Spanish *bota,* or wineskin (which is likely to be lined with plastic).

Antiques

You'll have to leave the tourist areas to find any amazing old trinkets at bargain prices. But even in a resort you may come across an appealing piece of old ironwork or hand carving at a relatively sensible price. At very least you can always take home a rusty old door

key suitable for a haunted house, or a kitchen iron of genuine pre-electric vintage.

Antique shopping is made easy in Barcelona, where many shops are concentrated in the ancient streets around the cathedral. Dealers carry antiques as well as reproductions of antiques; sometimes the dividing line becomes blurred.

Where to Shop

Prices in tourist resorts almost always exceed those in the big cities or inland towns.

Barcelona, with its fashionable shops, offers variety and quality, but no single street or neighbourhood will satisfy your window-shopping. The commercial area is so extensive that you might have to walk miles to compare quality and value.

Shopping Tips

Even so, try to price items in more than one shop before deciding. Prices tend to vary significantly from shop to shop.

Occasionally, you'll see a notice of sales—*rebajas* (or *rebaixes* in Catalan)—in shop windows. While legitimate sales do take place, usually at the end of the season to dispose of unsold stock, you'll have to be a bit cautious. Here, too, shopping around is the best way to find a bargain.

When you're spending a substantial amount at one shop, suggest a discount. Some store-owners may deduct up to ten percent, particularly on very large sales. But this is by no means the general rule.

The letters PVP on price-tags mean *precio de venta al público,* or retail price.

Museums

Barcelona alone counts more than 30 museums. This listing of Costa Dorada museums covers only those institutions of greatest general interest.

Most Spanish museums are open from Tuesday to Saturday from about 10 a.m. to 1.30 or 2 p.m., and 6 to 8 p.m., and Sundays from 10 a.m. to 2 p.m.; closed on Mondays and certain holidays.

Barcelona

Museo Arqueológico (Archaeological Museum). Art and relics dug up in the Barcelona area as well as elsewhere in Spain—prehistoric implements, Carthaginian necklaces, Roman mosaics (Calle Lérida, at the foot of Montjuich).

Museo de Arte de Cataluña (Museum of Catalonian Art). Top priority museum, with a beautifully arranged and displayed collection of medieval religious art, all housed in a mock palace (Palacio Nacional, Montjuich).

Museo de Cera (Wax Museum). This one is commercial and more expensive. Three hundred wax effigies of historical, contemporary and fictional figures (Rambla).

Colección Cambó (Cambó Collection). Paintings by Raphael and Titian, Goya and El Greco, Rubens and van Dyck, in an elegant 18th-century palace (Palacio de la Virreina).

Museo Picasso (Calle de Moncada, 15). From early scribblings to most mature

Barcelona boasts great collection of medieval art. Opposite: *shops sell antiques and original pottery.*

triumphs, the life's work of the great Spanish painter is laid out in two noble mansions of Old Barcelona.

Museo de Indumentaria (Costume Museum). More than 4,000 items showing the evolution of fashion from the 16th century to the present. (Calle de Moncada.)

Museo de Arte Moderno (Museum of Modern Art). Nineteenth and 20th-century paintings by Catalan artists in the Parque de la Ciudadela.

Museo Marítimo (Maritime Museum). Medieval shipyard (Atarazanas) converted into repository of full-sized and miniature souvenirs from the high seas.

Centro de Estudios de Arte Contemporáneo (or Centre d'Estudis d'Art Contemporani; Joan Miró Foundation). Modern paintings and sculptures exhibited in brilliant galleries and gardens in the Parque de Montjuich.

Museo Federico Marés (Federico Marés Museum). Right next to the Cathedral in Calle de los Condes de Barcelona, a vast collection of ancient religious sculptures.

Palacio de Pedralbes (Pedralbes Palace). 1920s palace fit for a king (Alfonso XIII).

Pueblo Español (Spanish Village). Instructive, imaginary all-Spanish town without children, dogs, or characters (on Montjuich).

Museo Militar (Military Museum). Military souvenirs—toy soldiers, real guns—in a mainly 18th-century fortress atop Montjuich.

Museo de Historia de la Ciudad (Museum of the History of the City). Built by chance right on top of Barcelona's richest archaeological digs in Plaza del Rey, this museum's skilfully lit basement is an archaeology lover's delight.

Museo del Monasterio de Pedralbes (Museum of the Monastery of Pedralbes). Main attraction of this museum is a collection of beautiful wall paintings by Ferrer Bassa from the 14th-century.

Tarragona

Museu Arqueològic (Archaeological Museum). Statues, mosaics and medaillons from Tarragona's Roman era. (Note: Adjoining **Pretori Romà** with additional ancient objects.)

Necròpoli i Museu Paleocristià (Necropolis and Paleo-Christian Museum). Tarragona's early Christians were buried in style and grace.

Passeig Arqueològic (Archaeological promenade). City walls and watch towers amid meticulously tended gardens. Open until midnight in summer. (Roman Forum, another outdoor attraction, also operates floodlit in summer.)

For Children

Barcelona Zoo. As pleasant and instructive a zoo as you'll find anywhere in the world.

Pueblo Español, Barcelona. Simulated Spanish town recreating architecture from all provinces in one slightly confusing ensemble. Watch a woodcarver chisel a statuette, a glassblower make a vase.

Rent-a-burro: how to make a child happy. The donkey's smiling, too.

Boat Trips. Round Barcelona harbour in a launch, for instance, for a close-up inspection of a busy port. Excursion firms also operate day-trips by bus and boat to Costa Brava.

Fun Fairs (Amusement Parks). Two big ones in Barcelona, in Montjuich and Tibidabo. Noise and gaiety along with fine views of the city and sea. Funiculars serve each.

Güell Park. Gaudí's zany whimsicality charms children, who especially admire his optical illusions. Free.

Barcelona Maritime Museum. The history of sailing, from Roman anchors to model of nuclear-propelled ship.

Santa María replica. Part of the Maritime Museum, a full-size model of Columbus's flagship is moored in the port nearby, available for boarding during the daytime.

Burro Safari. Travel agencies mobilize donkeys for tourist outings.

Tartana Excursions. A country trip in a horse-drawn cart, as devised by travel agencies.

Bloodless Bullfights. Mock *corridas* with baby bulls and audience participation. Some agencies include "champagne" and dancing.

Safari Excursion. Coach tours make a half-day outing to and through Rioleón Safari, where wild animals roam free. Near Vendrell (Tarragona).

Festivals

Religious and civic holidays are so frequent in Spain that the odds favour your witnessing a fiesta during your holiday, wherever you may be:

80 *Balloons and bouncing balls prove simple pleasures are usually best.*

February

Ametlla de Mar — *Fiestas de la Virgen de la Candalaria*. Religious procession, regatta.

Villanueva y Geltrú — *Fiestas de "Les Comparses"*. Folklore and "battle of sweets": 20 tons of sweets are consumed.

March or April

Montserrat
Poblet — *Semana Santa* (Holy Week) ceremonies. Processions and other observances in all towns.

April

Barcelona — *Fiesta de San Jorge y día de Cervantes*. St. George's Day, coinciding with Cervantes Day, a Book Fair, and the Day of Lovers. Animation and colour.

May

Badalona — *Fiestas de Primavera y San Anastasio*. Spring Festival and St. Anastasius' Day. Exhibition of roses.

Calella — *Fiestas de Primavera*. Spring Festival. Folk-dancing competition, old car parade, marching bands.

May or June

Sitges — *Fiesta del Corpus Christi*. Streets carpeted with flowers. Music, dancing, fireworks.

June

Calella — *"Aplec" de Sardanas*. Catalonia's most important folk-dance festival.

July

Arenys de Mar — *Fiesta mayor de San Zenón*. Celebrations asea and ashore. Folklore.

August

Valls — *Fiestas del Firagost* (Assumption). Harvest celebration, folklore, religious procession.

Vilafranca del Penedés — *Fiesta mayor de San Félix, mártir*. Religious procession. Folklore featuring "human castles".

September

Barcelona — *Fiestas de la Merced*. Theatre, music.

Tarragona — *Fiestas de Santa Tecla* (St. Thecla). Religious ans folkloric spectacles.

October

Sitges — *Fiesta de la Vendimia* (Grape-harvest festival). Tastings and dance.

Nightlife

Barcelona swings. So do the major resorts. Almost anywhere tourists alight along the Costa Dorada they find a conglomeration of bars, discothèques and *boîtes*. There's really no excuse except exhaustion for spending an evening slumped before the television in your hotel lounge.

Tour agencies along the coast run a Saturday-night excursion to Barcelona to admire the illuminated fountains of Montjuich and see Flamenco dancers in small specialized restaurants. There are two basic kinds of Flamenco (see p. 73), and the animated *cante chico* is the version usually performed in *tablaos*. Although Flamenco is essentially an art of Southern Spain and seen to its best effect there, Barcelona attracts many of the great performers.

Another excursion by coach takes in the most elegant floorshows in Barcelona. Normally the all-inclusive price includes dinner and a quota of drinks.

Organized barbecue evenings are a popular rustic substitute for the big-city nightclub tour. Travel agencies

take coachloads of tourists from the resorts to a regional beauty spot where plenty of food, wine and music are supplied.

Big and little towns along the coast have their discothèques and flamenco shows. In fine weather it's a novelty to escape from deafening smoke-filled rooms into deafening open-air nightspots. There is something special about dancing under the moon and stars.

Concerts, Opera, Ballet

Local or visiting orchestras and choirs provide a steady diet for Barcelona music-lovers.

The city's opera house, the Gran Teatro del Liceo, was described as the finest theatre in the world when it opened in 1857. Famous opera and ballet companies appear there every year. Most of its seats belong to subscribers, so it may be difficult for the casual ticket-hunter to obtain seats.

Major concerts also take place at the wildly *art nouveau* Palacio de la Música, stubbornly known in Catalan as Palau de la Música Catalana.

Recitals, including occasional jazz concerts, are held in the stark surroundings of the 14th-century Iglesia de Santa María del Mar.

Catalans are deeply dedicated to music, so you may chance upon a concert in any resort town—perhaps the local choir performing in the parish church or the town cinema.

Theatre, Films

Most of Barcelona's dozen theatres seem to specialize in musicals and farces, but straight plays—in Spanish or Catalan—are also presented.

Almost all the films shown commercially in Spain have been dubbed into Spanish. Depending on the location of the cinema and success of the film, the prices of seats vary (see p. 100).

Fiestas

Village fetes, which occur with great frequency, can provide rousing spectacles, music, folk dancing. But Spaniards are very casual about fireworks, so beware of the more explosive parts of town.

Night on the Costa Dorada: bars, discos, restaurants for all tastes.

Wining and Dining

When in Spain, try some Spanish food. This advice is not so ludicrous as it may seem. You could easily spend a fortnight's holiday on the Costa Dorada subsisting on the anonymous international food in your hotel. What a shame.

Spanish cooking varies drastically from region to region.*

To many visitors, a favourite dish is the Andalusian "liquid salad" *gazpacho* (pronounced gath-PAT-cho). This is a chilled, highly flavoured soup to which chopped tomatoes, peppers, cucumbers, onions and sippets (croutons) are added to taste—a rousing refresher on a hot summer day.

Another classic Spanish dish, *paella* (pronounced pie-ALE-

*For a comprehensive food list, ask at your bookshop for the Berlitz Spanish-English/ English-Spanish dictionary, or the Berlitz EUROPEAN MENU READER.

84

ya), originated just down the coast in Valencia. It's named after the black iron pan in which the saffron rice is cooked. To this the cook adds whatever inspires him at the moment—squid, sausage, shrimp, rabbit, chicken, mussels, onion, peppers, peas, beans, tomatoes, garlic... Authentically, *paella* is served at lunchtime, cooked to order (about half an hour). Some Spaniards consider it a first course; others dig into it for the whole meal.

Catalan Cuisine

Esqueixada (pronounced es-kay-SHA-da) is a stimulating salad of cod, beans, pickled onions and tomato.

Xató (pronounced sha-TO) *de Sitges* is a related, but more complicated salad including anchovies, tunny fish or cod and a hot sauce made of olive oil, vinegar, red pepper, diced anchovies, garlic and ground almonds.

Pa amb tomàquet goes well with any salad. Peasant-style bread, in huge slices, is smeared with fresh tomato and grilled; it comes out a sort of primitive cousin of a pizza.

Escudella is considered a winter-time dish, but out of season you may come across the hearty broth containing beans, pasta, a chunk of sausage and a slice of meatloaf.

Butifarra is one of several varieties of sausage much appreciated in Catalonia. One famous species of sausage comes from the town of Vich.

Rovellons are enormous wild mushrooms which mark the start of autumn on the Costa Dorada. They're cooked with garlic and parsley, eaten with sausage or alone.

Pollo al ast (barbecued chicken) is grilled and basted on the spit, usually outside a restaurant so that the aroma lures customers inside.

Riz parellada, a Costa Do-

Rushed from the farm, fruits and vegetables temptingly displayed.

rada refinement of *paella,* is a gourmand's dream. The kitchen will have removed all the shells and bones from the seafood and meat before this feast is cooked, so it can be gulped down without mess or delay.

Fish in general makes up a substantial part of the local diet. Mostly it is just grilled and served with a salad and fried potatoes. In more sophisticated restaurants, you'll be offered elaborate variations with subtle sauces. No matter how primitive or elegant the place, the raw materials are likely to be first-rate.

Romesco is the fish sauce from Tarragona, envied and imitated in other Costa Dorada towns. This red sauce tastes right at home beside the Mediterranean in the company of fried fish and shellfish. The cooks of Tarragona are very coy when asked for the recipe, but key ingredients would appear to be red pepper, olive oil, garlic, bread crumbs and ground almonds.

Calçotada, an even more provincial dish, comes from Valls—tender baby onions in what's claimed to be the most irresistible combination of vegetables, meat and spices in all of Catalonia.

Sweets: The pastries of the Costa Dorada will destroy your diet. Just look in a bakery window; you don't have to know the names. One is more delectable than the next, crowned with nuts, custard, dried fruits, meringue, chocolate or powder sugar.

Crema Catalana, made of eggs, sugar, milk and cinnamon, is cooked to a more solid consistency than its Spanish cousin, *flan,* and it has a caramel-glaze topping.

Breakfast

In Spain breakfast is an insignificant meal—just an eye-opener to keep one alive until a huge and late lunch. A typical Costa Dorada breakfast consists of a cup of coffee and pastry. Breakfast coffee *(café con leche)* is half coffee, half hot milk. If it tastes too foreign to you, many bars and restaurants stock milder instant coffee, as well. Also in deference to foreign habits, *desayuno completo* is now available in most hotels and some cafés: orange juice, eggs, toast and coffee.

Returning to the subject of breakfast pastry, two types are worth a try. *Ensaimadas* are large fluffy sweet rolls dusted with sugar, a Balearic islands speciality also popular in Catalonia. *Churros* are fritters, often made before your eyes by a contraption which shoots the batter into boiling oil. If you *don't* dunk *churros* in your coffee, everyone will stare. (*Churros* with very thick hot chocolate is a popular afternoon snack in Spain.)

Restaurants

All Spanish restaurants are officially graded by forks, not stars. One fork is the lowest grade, five forks the élite. But ratings are awarded according to the facilities available, not the quality of the food. Many forks on the door guarantee higher prices but not necessarily better cooking.

Spanish restaurants usually offer a *menú del día* (day's special). This usually lists three courses available with bread and wine at a reasonable set price. But the *menú* is not always a bargain; in fact, it might even work out to cost more than the sum of its parts. Add up the *à la carte* prices to be certain. On the other hand, in country or working-class restaurants, the *menú* is

often the favourite of the regular clients, and cheap.

Normally, menu prices are "all-inclusive"—including all taxes and service charge. But it's still customary to leave a tip. Five percent is acceptable, ten percent is generous.

All restaurants, for the record, announce that an official complaints book is available to dissatisfied clients.

All that food but too busy to eat: rush hour in a Barcelona kitchen.

Meal times tend to be later than in most European countries. Restaurants serve lunch from about 1 to 3.30 p.m. and dinner from about 8.30 to 11. **87**

Resort hotels may serve dinner earlier for the convenience of foreign guests.

One hint for economy: order *vino de la casa* (house wine). It may be served in an anonymous bottle, a colourful ceramic carafe or even in a mislabelled second-hand bottle. But it's almost bound to be tolerably good and will cost less than half the price of a brand-name bottle.

Foreign Restaurants

Barcelona is reasonably well provided with restaurants featuring foreign cuisines. They include French, Italian, German and Chinese restaurants. In addition Barcelona has many fine restaurants devoted to regional cooking from the various gourmet regions of Spain.

Most resort centres also have eating places aiming at foreign palates. The restaurants enjoy varying degrees of authenticity.

Bars and Cafés

Open-air cafés are one of the pleasures of the Costa Dorada. A cup of coffee buys you a ringside seat for as long as you care to dawdle.

Bar and café bills include service charges, but small tips are the custom. Prices are usually 10 or 15 percent higher if you're served at a table rather than at the bar.

Bodegas are wine-cellars. In resort towns many popular tourist bars have been designed to create the atmosphere of casks and barrels.

Merenderos are beach restaurants, serving simple but tasty food.

Tapas

A *tapa* is a bite-sized morsel of food—meatballs, olives, fried-fish chunks, shellfish, seafood, vegetable salad; it can be almost anything edible. The word *tapa* means "lid" and comes from the old custom of giving a bite of food with a drink, the food being served on a saucer covering the top of the glass like a lid. Nowadays, sadly, the custom of giving away the *tapa* is all but non-existent. But the idea of selling *tapas* is stronger than ever. Some bars, called *tascas,* specialize in the snack trade. Instead of sitting down to a formal meal in a restaurant you can wander into a *tapa* bar, point to the items you like and eat your way down the counter.

Vocabulary: *una tapa* is the bite-sized portion; *una ración* is a half-sized plateful; and *una porción* is a large helping. Caution: it's quite possible to spend more for a meal of *tapas* than for a good, conventional dinner.

Wines and Spirits

Both provinces of the Costa Dorada—Barcelona and Tarragona—produce good wine.

Priorato is a well-known red wine of the region. Tarragona wines are notable in white or rosé. Penedés can be red or white. In Sitges a dessert wine, malmsey (*malvasía* in Spanish), is produced. And the Penedés region is a major source of the world's best selling white sparkling wine, unofficially called Spanish *champán*.

Don't give a thought to "winemanship", or matching wits with the wine waiter to choose just the right vintage. When the average Spaniard sits down to a meal, he just orders *"vino"*, and it means *red* wine to the average waiter. Often served chilled, this house wine can go with fish or meat or anything. Relax and enjoy the unpretentiousness.

There is no social misdemeanour implied in diluting your wine if you wish, particularly on a hot day. The addition of *gaseosa*, a cheap fizzy lemonade, turns red wine into an imitation of *sangría*. (Real

As in all Mediterranean countries, outdoor cafés prosper in Catalonia. **89**

sangría, however, is a mixture of red wine, lemon and orange juice, brandy, mineral water, ice and slices of fruit—rather like punch and very popular in hot summer.)

If you're not in the mood for wine at all, have no qualms about ordering beer or a soft drink or mineral water. No one will turn up a snobbish nose.

You may consider Spanish brandy too heavy or sweet for your taste, compared with French cognac. But it's very cheap—often the same price as a soft drink.

A word about prices: if you insist on drinking imported Scotch or bourbon, expect to pay plenty. However, an enormous range of familiar spirits and liqueurs are available at very low prices because they are made under licence in Spain. Look around a wine shop to see just how cheap some brands are.

A last word to alert you to a non-alcoholic drink you might not have noticed. *Horchata de chufa* is a very Spanish refresher, possibly first imported by the Moors. It's made from a fruity, wrinkled little nut with a sweet taste, similar to an almond.

To help you order...

Could we have a table?	**¿Nos puede dar una mesa?**
Do you have a set menu?	**¿Tiene un menú del día?**
I'd like a/an/some...	**Quisiera...**

beer	**una cerveza**	milk	**leche**
bread	**pan**	mineral water	**agua mineral**
coffee	**un café**	napkin	**una servilleta**
condiments	**los condimentos**	potatoes	**patatas**
cutlery	**los cubiertos**	rice	**arroz**
dessert	**un postre**	salad	**una ensalada**
fish	**pescado**	sandwich	**un bocadillo**
fruit	**fruta**	soup	**una sopa**
glass	**un vaso**	sugar	**azúcar**
ice-cream	**un helado**	tea	**un té**
meat	**carne**	(iced) water	**agua (fresca)**
menu	**la carta**	wine	**vino**

...and read the menu

aceitunas	olives
ajo	garlic
albaricoques	apricots
albóndigas	meatballs
almejas	baby clams
anchoas	anchovies
anguila	eel
arroz	rice
asado	roast
atún	tunny (tuna)
bacalao	codfish
besugo	sea bream
bistec	beef steak
boquerones	fresh anchovies
caballa	mackerel
calamares (a la romana)	squid (deep fried)
callos	tripe
cangrejo	crab
caracoles	snails
cebollas	onions
cerdo	pork
champiñones	mushrooms
chorizo	a spicy pork sausage
chuleta	chops
cordero	lamb
dorada	sea-bass
ensalada	salad
entremeses	hors-d'oeuvre
estofado	stew
filete	fillet
flan	caramel mould
frambuesas	raspberries
fresas	strawberries
frito	fried
galletas	biscuits (cookies)
gambas	shrimp
granadas	pomegranates
guisantes	peas
helado	ice-cream
higos	figs
huevo	eggs
jamón	ham
judías	beans
langosta	spiny lobster
langostino	prawn
lenguado	sole
limón	lemon
lomo	loin
manzana	apple
mariscos	shellfish
mejillones	mussels
melocotón	peach
merluza	hake
naranja	orange
ostras	oysters
pastel	cake
pescado	fish
pescadilla	whiting
pez espada	swordfish
pimiento	green pepper
piña	pineapple
plátano	banana
pollo	chicken
postre	dessert
pulpitos	baby octopus
queso	cheese
salchichón	salami
salmonete	red mullet
salsa	sauce
sandía	watermelon
sopa	soup
ternera	veal
tortilla	omelet
tostada	toast
trucha	trout
uvas	grapes
verduras	vegetables

Sports and Other Activities

Facilities vary from zero along isolated stretches to the elaborate bars and changing rooms of the big resorts.

Deck-chairs and umbrellas can be hired everywhere for a reasonable price. Air mattresses *(li-lo)*, for sun-bathing and swimming, are another matter. It may well work out cheaper to buy your own for the season.

Vast sand beaches make the Costa Dorada a natural winner for holiday-makers inclined to water sports. The mild climate, moreover, extends the season for sports ashore. And if it should rain, the indoor sports provide exciting diversion, whether you play table tennis or watch Basques scoop up a bullet-fast *pelota*.

Here's a run-down of sports to choose from:

Beach Pursuits

Along much of the coast, golden sand slopes gently into a calm sea. The angle is less dependably gradual north-east of Barcelona; be alert for undercurrents. With few exceptions, lifeguards do not exist. But in many resorts first-aid stations are established on the main beaches.

Boating and Sailing

If you arrive in your own yacht, you'll find the facilities you need at any of these boating centres: Arenys de Mar, Barcelona, Garraf, Villanueva y Geltrú, Torredembarra, Tarragona, Salou, Cambrils, Amposta, San Carlos de la Rápita.

If you've left your yacht at home but would like to hire a boat on the spot, many resorts can come up with sailing boats. It usually depends upon local beach and sea conditions. Small fibre-glass dinghies are perfectly safe for sailing just off shore. If you plan to do much sailing on your holiday, try to negotiate a cheaper bulk rate.

ing on a surfboard powered by a hand-held sail.

For the less adventurous or less affluent, there remains the *pedalo* (paddle boat). This sea-borne bicycle built for two can

Down to the sea in bathing suits, or all rigged up in a parachute to keep up with latest holiday sport.

A recent development combines the speed of sailing with the thrills of tight-rope walking. "Windsurfing" involves skimming over the sea balanc-

be as unglamorous as an 1890s bathing costume, but it will take you far from the crowds. Expensive enough—check before you embark. **93**

Water-Skiing

Increased fuel costs have pushed this sport into the luxury class.

In some resorts, an exciting airborne variation—kite-skiing —is attracting great attention. Definitely not for the faint-hearted.

Fishing

In all resorts inexpensive rods and reels arc sold.

Deep-sea-style fishing is a logistical problem; if you can organize a group you may be able to hire a boat. There are no facilities for renting equipment.

For all information and licences, consult the local office of the Instituto Nacional para la Conservación de la Naturaleza (ICONA):

Barcelona: Carrer Sabino de Arana, 22.

Tarragona: Avda. de Catalunya, 22-E.

Underwater Fishing

This increasingly popular sport requires a licence, issued by the local Comandancia de Marina (Maritime Authorities). You may use a snorkel tube and mask along with mechanical harpoon. Underwater fishing with scuba oxygen equipment or air guns is strictly not allowed. Incidentally, if you should come upon archaeological relics in your undersea travels, remember that it is forbidden to collect these specimens.

Golf

Four golf courses are open all-year-round on the Costa Dorada, mostly near Barcelona.

- Real Club de Golf El Prat,

Tennis

Many hotels along the coast either have their own courts or can provide access for their guests to a local tennis club. For fees, see p. 100.

The Spanish sun is shining for the fishers on the quayside as for sedate golfers on the beautiful green near Barcelona.

in Prat de Llobregat (near Barcelona airport). 27 holes.
- Club de Golf Llavaneras, San Andrés de Llavaneras, near Mataró. Nine holes.
- Club de Golf de San Cugat, near San Cugat del Vallés. 18 holes.
- Club de Golf Terramar, Sitges. Nine holes.

Horse-Riding

Some resort travel agencies advertise riding excursions. For a set fee they provide transport to and from a ranch, two and a half hours of riding, and a country meal. If you make your own way to a stable the rates are much lower.

95

Hunting and Shooting

Two areas of unusual interest for hunters in the southern part of Catalonia: the Ebro Delta and the rugged mountain zone west of Tortosa.

The Ebro Delta, the marshy peninsula facing Amposta, is considered one of the dozen best waterfowl spots in Spain, and Spain claims Europe's best

Tortosa and Beceite passes. This is one of the refuges of the Spanish mountain goat, a rare species in modern times. Hunting there is very severely controlled.

Otherwise, the Costa Dorada area is inhabited by unexceptional quantities of rabbit, hare and partridge. The small game season opens on October 12 and closes in February.

waterfowl hunting. The season begins in October and lasts to mid-March. For information and the actual hunting licence apply to the Instituto Nacional para la Conservación de la Naturaleza (ICONA), Avda. de Catalunya, 22-E, Tarragona.

The same ICONA office can answer your questions on the national hunting reserve of the

Skiing

Yes, skiing—on snow. Sophisticated winter resorts flourish from December to April in the Catalonian Pyrenees, within a hundred miles or so of Barcelona. The Ministry of Information and Tourism issues a detailed booklet on winter sports in Spain.

Just Looking

Among spectator sports, football is Spain's greatest passion. Barcelona supports two major teams—Español and Barcelona (affectionately known as *Barça*). *Barça's* stadium can seat about 90,000 spectators—almost the entire population of Tarragona

Popular indoor spots are

For a rousingly different experience, go to a *frontón* to watch the Basque ball game, *pelota,* called in Basque *jai-alai.* You'll catch on to the rules fairly early in the game, though the betting system which engrosses most of the audience may remain mysterious. Bookies in blue jackets negotiate with their clients by hand signals and slang, transmitting

Jai-alai *speed-merchants* (opposite) *thrill the crowds. Some* (above) *prefer a slower pace.*

basketball, boxing and wrestling.

Greyhounds *(galgos)* race at various *canódromos.* Betting is permitted.

receipts inside tennis balls. Even the referee, on the dangerous side of the protective fence, has been known to place a discreet bet during the match. The tireless players use woven straw scoops to combine the functions of glove and catapult, snagging the whizzing ball and blasting it back against the far wall.

How to Get There

From Great Britain

BY AIR: There are daily, non-stop flights to Barcelona from London and Dublin. The journey takes approximately two hours. Services from provincial airports are generally routed via London.

There are several fares to choose from. The Economy fare offers reductions to youths under 21 and students under 26. Budget fares are available but have a 50% cancellation charge. You can also travel on an Excursion fare, valid for between 7 and 91 days. Tickets for Excursion fares must be reserved and paid for at the same time, and there is a surcharge for cancellations. A special, one-month Excursion fare allows you to return whenever you like, so long as you spend at least one Saturday night in Barcelona. All these fares have reductions for children.

Charter Flights and Package Tours: Many companies operate all-in package tours, which include flight, hotel and meals; check carefully to make sure that you are not liable to any surcharges. Most agents recommend a modestly-priced cancellation insurance, which protects you if you are unable to travel due to illness.

If you prefer to arrange your own accommodation and do not mind having to restrict your holiday to either one or two weeks, you can take advantage of the many charter flights that are available.

BY ROAD: The principal cross-channel car ferries operate from Dover and Folkestone to Calais and Boulogne. There are also ferries from Dover to Dunkerque, Portsmouth to Cherbourg or Le Havre, Southampton to Cherbourg or Le Havre, and Newhaven to Dieppe. Hovercrafts travel from Dover and Ramsgate to Boulogne and Calais and take only 35 minutes.

The route via Paris is almost entirely toll motorway to Barcelona.

Coaches leave London daily for Barcelona—a journey of 25 hours. This is relatively cheap but somewhat exhausting.

BY RAIL: There are crowded but efficient trains from Great Britain to Spain. Sleeper reservations are recommended and must be made in advance.

Anyone under 26 or over 65 can purchase an Inter-Rail card, valid for one month's unlimited rail travel in participating European countries.

From North America

BY AIR: Direct daily flights to Barcelona leave from two American cities: New York (with a stopover in Madrid en route) and San Francisco (with a change of planes in New York). Barcelona is easily reached from more than 60 cities via daily connecting flights. In addition, another 20 cities have connecting flights to Barcelona on certain days of the week. However, the greatest number of flights operate to Madrid from New York and Miami. Major Canadian cities offer daily connecting service, using major European gateway cities.

The 7-to-180-day APEX (Advance Purchase Excursion) fare must be paid for 21 days prior to departure. If the reservation is cancelled or changed, a $50 penalty is charged. Stopovers are not permitted. Children fly for two-thirds of the adult fare (or 10% under the age of two years). The 30-to-365-day Excursion ticket must be purchased at the time the reservation is made, but the return flight may be booked at any time. The prices of APEX and Excursion fares vary according to the season.

Charter Flights and Package Tours: Most charter flights operate to Madrid or the Costa del Sol. If extensions are offered, it is possible to visit the Costa Dorada independently. Barcelona is often featured on package tours combining Majorca or the Costa del Sol.

When to Go

Sunbathers enjoy the beaches of the Costa Dorada for about six months of the year; the rest of the time the mild climate still provides a pleasant break for visitors from northern Europe.

Except for July and August, when the heat rarely abates, the nights can turn unexpectedly chilly.

The accompanying chart deals specifically with the climate of Barcelona, damper than Tarragona and intermediate beach areas.

		J	F	M	A	M	J	J	A	S	O	N	D
Air temperature	°F	55	52	60	65	73	76	82	83	77	69	62	59
(maximum)	°C	12	11	15	17	22	24	27	27	24	20	16	14
Air temperature	°F	44	41	47	45	58	64	68	69	64	59	50	48
(minimum)	°C	6	4	8	7	14	17	19	20	17	14	10	8

All figures shown are approximate monthly averages.

Planning Your Budget

To give you an idea of what to expect, here are some average prices in Spanish pesetas (ptas.). However, remember that all prices must be regarded as approximate, as inflation creeps relentlessly up.

Baby-sitters. 150–300 ptas. per hour.

Camping. 150–250 ptas. per person per night (100–150 ptas. per child), 150–250 ptas. per tent or car, 200–400 ptas. for caravan (trailer), 125–400 ptas. for motorcycle, depending on category of site.

Car hire. *Seat 127* 1,250 ptas. per day, 11.50 ptas. per km., 17,500 ptas. per week (unlimited mileage). *Seat 124 D* 1,575 ptas. per day, 14.50 ptas. per km., 23,000 ptas. per week (unlimited mileage). *Seat 131* 2,250 ptas. per day, 20 ptas. per km., 32,550 ptas. per week (unlimited mileage). Add 3% tax.

Cigarettes. Spanish 20–50 ptas., foreign brands 80 ptas. and up.

Entertainment. *Cinema* in resorts 50–150 ptas., Barcelona 200 ptas. *Theatre* tickets 350 ptas. and up, *Museums* 50–150 ptas.

Guides and interpreters. 1,500 ptas. (1–5 people) for half-day, 2,000 ptas. for Sundays and holidays, 100 ptas. for each additional person.

Hairdressers. *Man's* haircut 500 ptas. *Woman's* shampoo and set 500 ptas., blow-dry 500 ptas., manicure 200 ptas.

Hotels (double room with bath). ***** 6,000 ptas., **** 4,000 ptas., *** 2,500 ptas., ** 1,800 ptas., * 1,000 ptas., *Youth hostel* 700 ptas.

Laundry. Shirt 70 ptas., blouse 80 ptas., pyjamas 90 ptas. *Dry-cleaning:* man's jacket 200 ptas., trousers 150 ptas., suit 350 ptas., dress 200 ptas., skirt 150 ptas., blouse 80 ptas. *Launderette:* 5 kg. load 200 ptas.

Meals and drinks. Continental breakfast 125 ptas., *plato del día* 250 ptas., beer 30 ptas., brandy (Spanish) 50 ptas., coffee 30 ptas., soft drink 25 ptas.

Metro. 20 ptas. weekdays, a book of ten tickets 150 ptas.

Sports. *Golf* (use of course) 800–1,000 ptas. per day, instruction 1,000–1,500 ptas., caddies 600–1,000 ptas., *tennis* 300 ptas. per hour, court fee 200 ptas., tuition 700 ptas. *water–skiing* (15-min. run) 400–600 ptas., *windsurfing* 700 ptas. per hour.

Taxis. Initial charge 45 ptas., 25 ptas. per km., waiting charge per hour 645 ptas., 15 ptas. per piece of luggage.

Trains (sample fares, return). Barcelona–Calella 150 ptas., Barcelona–Sitges 90 ptas.

BLUEPRINT for a Perfect Trip

An A-Z Summary of Practical Information and Facts

Contents

A star (*) following an entry indicates that relevant prices are to be found on page 100.

Listed after some basic entries is the appropriate Spanish translation, usually in the singular, plus a number of phrases that should help you when seeking assistance.

Although every effort has been made to ensure the accuracy of the information contained in this book, changes will inevitably occur, and we would be pleased to hear of any new developments.

A **AIRPORT** *(aeropuerto)*. Barcelona's modern international airport, along the sea at Prat de Llobregat, is only about 15 kilometres from the centre of the city. Porters are available to carry your bags to the taxi rank or bus stop; free baggage trolleys also are at passengers' disposal. A tourist information office, car hire agencies, souvenir shops, a currency exchange office and a duty-free shop operate here.

Buses link the airport with the town terminal at Plaza de España, a 20-minute trip.

The Spanish Railways operate a link between the airport and Sants station in western Barcelona. Trains run every 15 minutes, and the trip takes only 11 minutes.

Charter flights for resorts near Tarragona often use the military airfield at Reus. Tour operators provide ground transportation.

Where's the bus for…?	**¿De dónde sale el autobús para…?**
What time does the bus leave for…?	**¿A qué hora sale el autobús para…?**
Porter!	**¡Mozo!**

B **BABY-SITTERS*** *(señorita para cuidar niños)*. This service can usually be arranged with your hotel. Rates can vary considerably but are generally lower in the quieter resort areas; in most places they go up after midnight.

Can you get me a baby-sitter for tonight?	**¿Puede conseguirme una señorita para cuidar los niños esta noche?**

BICYCLE and MOTORSCOOTER HIRE *(bicicletas/scooters de alquiler)*. In a few resorts, bicycles—including tandem models—may be hired by the hour or by the day. You may also be able to find a garage which will rent you a moped by the day or week. However, these 49-cc. machines are a less-than-carefree mode of transport on resort-area roads, especially in season when traffic is extremely heavy. Motorscooters of 150 to 175-cc., powerful enough for a driver and a passenger, cost almost as much to hire as a car. Be prepared to lay out a deposit. Remember that use of crash helmets is compulsory, whatever the capacity of the engine.

I'd like to hire a bicycle.	**Quisiera alquilar una bicicleta.**
What's the charge per day/week?	**¿Cuánto cobran por día/semana?**

CAMPING* *(camping).* The Costa Dorada has more officially approved campsites than any other resort area in Spain. Facilities vary according to the classification, but most have electricity and running water. Some have shops, small playgrounds for children, restaurants, swimming pools—even launderettes. For a complete list of camp-sites, consult any Spanish National Tourist Office (see TOURIST INFORMATION OFFICES), or write to Agrupación Nacional de Cam-pings de España (ANCE):

Duque de Medinaceli, 2, Madrid

May we camp here?	**¿Podemos acampar aquí?**
We have a tent/caravan (trailer).	**Tenemos una tienda de camping/una caravana.**

CAR HIRE* *(coches de alquiler).* See also DRIVING. There are car hire firms in the main towns and tourist resorts. The most common type of car available for hire is the *Seat,* the Spanish version of the Italian *Fiat.* The rates given on page 101 are sample prices of major operators; local firms may charge somewhat less.

A deposit, as well as advance payment of the estimated rental charge, is generally required, although holders of major credit cards are normally exempt from this. A tax of 3% is added to the total; third-party insurance is automatically included.

Normally you must be over 21 to hire a car. You should have an International Driving Licence, but many firms accept a valid licence from your country of residence. You'll *probably* get away with the latter if stopped by the police, but there is a risk.

I'd like to rent a car (tomorrow).	**Quisiera alquilar un coche (para mañana).**
for one day/a week	**por un día/una semana**
Please include full insurance coverage.	**Haga el favor de incluir el seguro todo riesgo.**

C **CIGARETTES, CIGARS, TOBACCO*** *(cigarrillos, puros, tabaco).*
Most Spanish cigarettes are made of strong, black tobacco with a high
nicotine content. Imported foreign brands are up to three times the
price of local makes, though foreign brands produced in Spain under
licence can be cheaper than when bought at home. Locally made
cigars are cheap and reasonably good. Canary Island cigars are excellent and Cuban cigars are readily available. Pipe smokers find the
local tobacco somewhat rough.

Tabacalera S.A. is the government tobacco monopoly: they supply
their official shops, *estancos,* who supply everybody else. Cigarette
shops often sell postage stamps, too.

A packet of…/A box of matches, please.	**Un paquete de…/Una caja de cerillas, por favor.**
filter-tipped	**con filtro**
without filter	**sin filtro**

CLOTHING. Whatever you wear for hot north European summers
will be fine for the Costa Dorada. By day between July and early
September you'll be very unlucky to need a wrap, but have one handy
in the evenings. In other months, especially between November and
March, winds can sometimes blow cold, so always carry a jacket or
coat. Even in August you'll need a warm covering in the mountains.
When visiting churches women no longer *have* to cover their heads,
but decent dress is certainly expected.

COMMUNICATIONS. Post offices *(correos)* are for mail and telegrams only; normally you can't make telephone calls from them.

Post office hours. 9 a.m. to 1 or 2 p.m. and 4 or 5 to 6 or 7 p.m. Monday to Friday, mornings only on Saturdays. Barcelona's main post
office is open from 9 a.m. to 2 p.m. and 4 to 6 p.m. daily in summer,
9 a.m. to 9 p.m. in winter.

Mail. If you don't know in advance where you'll be staying, you can
have your mail addressed to the *Lista de Correos* (poste restante or
general delivery) in the nearest town. Take your passport to the post
office as identification and be prepared to pay a small fee for each
letter received.

Postage stamps are also on sale at tobacconists *(tabacalera* or *estan-*

104 *co)* and often at hotel desks.

Mail boxes marked *extranjero* are for foreign-destination mail. If the box is unmarked, it's good for all addresses.

Telegrams *(telegrama)*. Telegram and post office counter services work independent hours and usually overlap. Times vary from town to town, too, but you can always send telegrams by phone—dial 322 20 00.

The telegraph section in the main post offices of major cities stays open 24 hours a day. If you are staying at a hotel, the receptionist can take telegrams. Telex service is also available in principal post offices.

Telephone *(teléfono)*. Telephone offices, marked by a blue and white sign, are almost always independent of the post office. Most now have automatic dialling facilities for local, inter-urban and some international calls. Area or STD code numbers are given on charts in each booth in the office. Ask the operator if in trouble. You'll get a bill at the end of your call, worked out by the operator's meter.

Street telephone booths and kiosks are springing up everywhere, sometimes replacing exchanges. Old ones require 1-peseta pieces, or, in the oldest, tokens *(fichas)* bought from a bar or café. New models use 5-, 25- and 50-peseta coins. You line them up on the ledge provided and the machine helps itself. Hold on to the leading coin when you hang up, as the machine sometimes takes a last gulp. To reverse the charges, ask for *cobro revertido*. For a personal (person-to-person) call, specify *persona a persona*.

Can you get me this number in…?	**¿Puede comunicarme con este número en…?**
Have you received any mail for…?	**¿Ha recibido correo para…?**
A stamp for this letter/postcard, please.	**Por favor, un sello para esta carta/tarjeta.**
express (special delivery)	**urgente**
airmail	**vía aérea**
registered	**certificado**
I want to send a telegram to…	**Quisiera mandar un telegrama a…**

COMPLAINTS. By law, all hotels and restaurants must have official complaint forms *(hoja de reclamaciones)* and produce them on demand. The original of this triplicate document should be sent to the regional office of the Ministry of Tourism, one copy remains with the establishment complained against and you keep the third sheet. Merely asking for a complaint form is usually enough to resolve most matters since tourism authorities take a serious view of complaints and your host wants to keep both his reputation and his licence.

In the rare event of major obstruction, when it is not possible to call in the police, write directly to the Subsecretario del Turismo, Sección de Inspección y Reclamaciones:

Alcalá, 44, Madrid

If your problem is bad merchandise or car repairs, remember that in Spain consumer protection is in its early days. Seek out the owner or manager if you really think you've been wronged. Failing that, the local tourist office may help. In outrageous cases go to the police. Even if they cannot help, they'll be able to take action if they receive several complaints against any one firm.

CONSULATES *(consulado)*

Barcelona:

Eire. Gran Vía Carlos III, 94. 10th floor ; tel. 330 97 05

South Africa. Plaza Medinaceli, 4; tel. 318 42 58

U.K.* Avinguda Diagonal, 477; tel. 322 21 51

U.S.A. Vía Layetana, 33; tel. 319 95 50

Tarragona:

U.K.* Santián, 4; tel. 204 12 46

Almost all Western European countries have consulates in Barcelona. All embassies are located in Madrid.

If you run into trouble with authorities or the police, ask your consulate for advice.

Where is the American/British consulate?	**¿Dónde está el consulado americano/británico?**
It's very urgent.	**Es muy urgente.**

CONVERTER CHARTS. For fluid and distance measures, see page 109. Spain uses the metric system.

----

* Also for citizens of Commonwealth countries.

Temperature

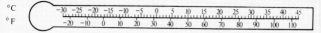

Length

Weight

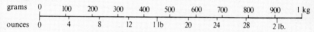

CRIME and THEFT. Spain's crime rate is low compared with most countries, but thefts and break-ins are increasing. Hang on to purses and wallets, especially in busy places—the bullfight, open air markets, fiestas. Don't take valuables to the beach. Lock cars and *never* leave cases, cameras, etc., on view. If you suffer a theft or break-in, report it to the Guardia Civil. You may not get your property back, but you'll help police build up a picture of local crime.

I want to report a theft.	**Quiero denunciar un robo.**
My ticket/wallet/passport has been stolen.	**Me han robado el billete/ la cartera/el pasaporte.**

DRIVING IN SPAIN

Entering Spain. To bring your car into Spain you will require:

International driving licence	Car registration papers	Green Card (an extension to your regular insurance policy, making it valid for foreign countries)
Recommended: a Spanish bail bond. If you injure somebody in an accident in Spain, you can be jailed while the accident is being investigated. This bond will bail you out. Apply to your insurance company.		

D A nationality sticker must be prominently displayed on the back of your car. Seat belts are compulsory. Not using them outside towns makes you liable to a stiff fine. A red reflecting warning triangle is compulsory when driving on motorways (expressways). Motorcycle riders and their passengers must wear crash helmets.

Driving conditions. Drive on the right. Pass on the left. Yield right of way to all traffic coming from the right. Spanish drivers tend to use their horn when passing other vehicles.

Main roads are adequate to very good and improving all the time. Secondary roads can be bumpy. The main danger of driving in Spain comes from impatience, especially on busy roads. A large percentage of accidents in Spain occur when passing, so take it easy. Wait until you have a long, unobstructed view.

Spanish truck and lorry drivers will often wave you on (by hand or by flashing their right directional signal) if it's clear ahead.

On country roads, beware of donkey and mule riders and horse-drawn carts. In villages, remember that the car only became a part of the Spanish way of life some 20 years ago; the villages aren't designed for them, and the older people are still not quite used to them. Drive with extra care to avoid children darting out of doorways and older folk strolling in the middle of the road, particularly after dark.

Beware, too, of that delicious but oh-so-heavy Spanish wine: the drinking and driving laws have been tightened up considerably, and fines are truly horrible!

Speed limits

A) Motorways (expressways) 120 k.p.h. (75 m.p.h.), caravans (trailers) 80 k.p.h. (50 m.p.h.).

B) main roads with two or more lanes in each direction or a lane for slow vehicles 100 k.p.h. (62 m.p.h.), caravans 80 k.p.h.

C) other roads 90 k.p.h.; caravans 70 k.p.h. (43 m.p.h).

D) in towns and villages 60 k.p.h. (36 m.p.h.).

"B" and "C" can be exceeded by 20 k.p.h. (12 m.p.h.) to overtake, provided the vehicle being overtaken is not travelling at the maximum permitted speed. "A" and "D" cannot be exceeded under any circumstances.

Traffic Police. The armed Civil Guard *(Guardia Civil)* patrols the highways on powerful black motorcycles. Always in pairs, these capable-looking characters are courteous, good mechanics and will stop to help anyone in trouble. They are severe on lawbreakers.

If fined, you may be expected to pay on the spot. The most frequent offences include passing without flashing directional-indicator lights, travelling too close to the car ahead and driving with a burnt-out head or tail light. (Spanish law requires you to carry a set of spare bulbs at all times.)

Parking. Many towns charge a token fee for parking during working hours; the cities more. The attendants are often disabled, and it's usual to round off the price of the ticket upwards.

Fuel and oil. Fuel is theoretically available in three grades—90, 96 and 98 octane—but not every petrol station carries the full range.

Fluid measures

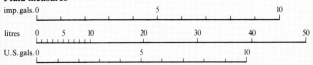

Distance

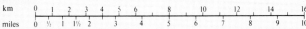

Breakdowns. Spanish garages are as efficient as any, and a breakdown will probably be cheaper to repair in Spain than in your home country. Spare parts are readily available for Spanish-built cars—*Seat* (the Spanish-licensed version of *Fiat*), *Renault*, *Simca*, *Dodge*, *Citroën*, *Morris* and *Austin Minis* and *1100*s. But spares for other makes may be hard to obtain. Make sure your car is in top shape before leaving home.

Road signs. Most road signs are the standard pictographs used throughout Europe. However, you may encounter these written signs:

¡Alto!	Stop!
Aparcamiento	Parking
Autopista (de peaje)	(Toll) motorway (expressway)
Ceda el paso	Give way (Yield)
Cruce peligroso	Dangerous crossroads
Cuidado	Caution
Despacio	Slow
Desviación	Diversion (Detour)
Peligro	Danger

D | **Prohibido adelantar** | No overtaking (passing)
| **Prohibido aparcar** | No parking
| **Puesto de socorro** | First-aid post

(International) Driving Licence | **Carné de conducir (internacional)**
Car registration papers | **Certificado de matrícula**
Green Card | **Carta verde**

Are we on the right road for...? | **¿Es ésta la carretera hacia...?**
Full tank, please, top grade. | **Llénelo, por favor, con super.**
Check the oil/tires/battery. | **Por favor, controle el aceite/los neumáticos/la batería.**

I've had a breakdown. | **Mi coche se ha estropeado.**
There's been an accident. | **Ha habido un accidente.**

DRUGS. The Spanish police have no sympathy for narcotics of any sort, or their users. Possession can be considered as evidence of intent to traffic, and the minimum sentence is six months (and may go up to 20 years).

E | **ELECTRIC CURRENT** *(corriente eléctrica).* Today 220-volt A.C. is becoming standard, but older installations of 125 volts can still be found. Check before plugging in. If the voltage is 125, American appliances (e.g. razors) built for 60 cycles will run on 50-cycle European current, but more slowly.

If you have trouble with any of your appliances ask your hotel receptionist to recommend an *electricista.*

What's the voltage—125 or 220? | **¿Cuál es el voltaje—ciento-veinticinco (125) o doscientos veinte (220)?**

an adaptor/a battery | **un adaptador/una pila**

EMERGENCIES. If you're not staying at a hotel, dial the police emergency number—091. You can always visit the local Municipal Police or the Guardia Civil. If possible take a Spanish speaker with you. Depending on the nature of the emergency, refer to the separate entries in this book, such as CONSULATES, MEDICAL CARE, POLICE, etc.

Though we hope you'll never need them, here are a few key words you might like to learn in advance:

Careful	**Cuidado**	Police	**Policía**
Fire	**Fuego**	Stop	**Deténgase**
Help	**Socorro**	Stop thief	**Al ladrón**

ENTRY and CUSTOMS FORMALITIES *(aduana)*. Citizens of Great **E**
Britain, the U.S.A., Canada and Eire need only a valid passport to
visit Spain, and even this requirement is waived for the British, who
may enter on the simplified Visitor's Passport. Though residents of
Europe and North America aren't subject to any health requirements,
visitors from further afield should check with a travel agent before
departure in case inoculation certificates are called for.

Visitors from Australia, New Zealand and South Africa need visas.

The following chart shows what main duty-free items you may take
into Spain and, when returning home, into your own country:

Into:	Cigarettes	Cigars	Tobacco	Spirits	Wine
Spain*	200 (400)	50 (100)	250 g. (500 g.)	1 l. or 2 l.	
Australia	200	or 250 g. or	250 g.	1 l. or	1 l.
Canada	200	and 50 and	900 g.	1.1 l. or	1.1 l.
Eire	200	or 50 or	250 g.	1 l. and	2 l.
N. Zealand	200	or 50 or	½ lb.	1 qt. and	1 qt.
S. Africa	400	and 50 and	250 g.	1 l. and	1 l.
U.K.	200	or 50 or	250 g.	1 l. and	2 l.
U.S.A.	200	and 100 and	**	1 l. or	1 l.

* The figures in parentheses are for non-European visitors only.
** A reasonable quantity.

You are also permitted personal clothing, jewellery and perfume, a
still camera with accessories and five rolls of film, a cine-camera and
five rolls of film, a pair of binoculars, etc. You may have to sign a
guarantee that you won't sell certain items in your possession while in
Spain, otherwise you may have to put up a deposit.

Currency restrictions: While there's no limit for the tourist on the
import or export of foreign currencies or traveller's cheques, you can't
bring in more than 100,000 pesetas, which should be declared to customs on arrival, or leave the country with more than 20,000 pesetas.

I've nothing to declare.   **No tengo nada que declarar.**
It's for my personal use.   **Es para mi uso personal.**   111

G   **GUIDES*** *(guía)*. Local tourist offices, hotels and travel agencies can put you in touch with qualified guides and interpreters if you want a personally directed tour or help in business negotiations.

We'd like an English-speaking guide.	**Queremos un guía que hable inglés**
I need an English interpreter.	**Necesito un intérprete de inglés.**

H   **HAIRDRESSERS*** *(peluquería)* and **BARBERS** *(barbería)*. Many hotels have their own salons, and the standard is generally good. Prices vary widely according to the class of establishment, but rates are often displayed in the window.

Not too much off (here).	**No corte mucho (aquí)**
A little more off (here).	**Un poco más (aquí).**
haircut	**corte**
shampoo and set	**lavado y marcado**
blow-dry	**modelado**
permanent wave	**permanente**
a colour rinse/hair-dye	**champú colorante/tinte**
a colour chart	**un muestrario**

HITCH-HIKING *(auto-stop)*. In Spain, hitch-hiking is permitted everywhere and is on the whole safe—which does not mean that it is necessarily easy! Waiting under that unblinking sun can be a thirsty business, interspersed with moments of despair... Best hitch-hike in pairs; girls have a better chance in this "game". If you sleep out in the open, don't bed down close to camping and caravan (trailer) sites. Police passing the campsite may awaken you to check your identity.

Can you give me/us a lift to...?	**¿Puede llevarme/llevarnos a...?**

HOTELS and ACCOMMODATION* *(hotel; alojamiento)*. Spanish hotel prices are no longer government-controlled. Prices range from a few hundred pesetas per night for a simple but always clean double room in a village *fonda* (inn) to several thousand pesetas for a double in a luxurious five star hotel. Before the guest takes a room he fills out a form with hotel category, room number and price and signs it. Breakfast is almost always charged for, whether taken or not.

    When you check into your hotel you might have to leave your passport at the desk. Don't worry, you'll get it back in the morning.

Other accommodation:

Hostal and **Hotel-Residencia.** Modest hotels, often family concerns, also graded by stars. A three-star *hostal* usually costs about the same as a two-star hotel, and so on down the scale.

Pensión. Boarding house, few amenities.

Fonda. Village inn, clean and unpretentious.

Parador. State-run inns, often in beautifully restored old buildings and often in isolated or little developed areas; good value for money.

Albergue de Juventud. There are youth hostels for boys and girls in Arenys de Mar, for boys only in Barcelona and Tarragona. During the tourist season it is wise to book in advance.

a single/double room	**una habitación sencilla/doble**
with bath/shower	**con baño/ducha**
What's the rate per night?	**¿Cual es el precio por noche?**

HOURS. Schedules here revolve around the siesta, one of the really great Spanish discoveries, aimed at keeping people out of the midday sun. The word has become universal; unfortunately, the custom hasn't. But when in Spain you should certainly try it.

To accommodate the midday pause, most shops and offices open from 9 a.m. to 1 p.m. and then from 4 p.m. to 8 p.m. Restaurants start serving lunch about 1 p.m. and dinner between 8 and 10 p.m.

LANGUAGE. The official language of Spain, Castilian, is understood everywhere on the Costa Dorada. However, a related Romance language, Catalan, is the native language of the people of Catalonia. Since the death of General Franco, there has been an immense increase in the use of Catalan. Frowned upon under El Caudillo, it has now taken its place as the second official language, and many Catalans express themselves more freely—and more willingly—in Catalan than in Spanish. On a brief visit to the Costa Dorada, your elementary Spanish will suffice, even if a few words of Catalan will always be appreciated.

For geographical reasons, the French language is widely understood and admired in Catalonia. In tourist areas, English and German are spoken as well. See also MAPS AND STREET NAMES.

	Catalan	Castilian
Good morning	*Bon dia*	*Buenos días*
Good afternoon	*Bones tardes*	*Buenas tardes*

L	Good night	*Bona nit*	*Buenas noches*
	Thank you	*Gràcies*	*Gracias*
	You're welcome	*De res*	*De nada*
	Please	*Si us plau*	*Por favor*
	Goodbye	*Adéu*	*Adiós*

The Berlitz phrase book SPANISH FOR TRAVELLERS covers most situations you are likely to encounter during your travels in Spain. The Berlitz Spanish-English/English-Spanish pocket dictionary contains 12,500 concepts, plus a menu-reader supplement.

Do you speak English?	**¿Habla usted inglés?**
I don't speak Spanish.	**No hablo español.**

LAUNDRY *(lavandería)* **and DRY-CLEANING** *(tintorería)*. Most hotels will handle laundry and dry-cleaning, but they'll usually charge more than a laundry or a dry-cleaners. For still greater savings, you can try a do-it-yourself launderette *(launderama)*.

Wher's the nearest laundry/dry-cleaners?	**¿Dónde está la lavandería/ tintorería más cercana?**
When will it be ready?	**¿Cuándo estará lista?**
I must have this for tomorrow morning.	**La necesito para mañana por la mañana.**

LOST PROPERTY. The first thing to do when you discover you've lost something is, obviously, to retrace your steps. If nothing comes to light, report the loss to the Municipal Police or the Guardia Civil.

I've lost my wallet/handbag/ passport.	**He perdido mi cartera/bolso/ pasaporte.**

M **MAPS and STREET NAMES.** Spain has been undergoing a formidable upheaval in many domains since 1975. One manifestation is in the names of streets, many of which are being re-baptised, causing a tourist considerable confusion.

Places now sometimes have two names, an old and a new one that bear no resemblance to each other; one may be Castilian, the other Catalan; one may pay honour to a hero of the Franco period, one a Catalan hero of history.

Maps cannot always keep up with this rapid evolution, so, with the above in mind, it's worth enquiring immediately of a local inhabitant if you can't find a certain street you're looking for. We have given **114** "new" names whenever possible.

A tip to help recognize the new place names:

Castilian	English	Catalan
Avenida	Avenue	*Avinguda*
Calle	Street	*Carrer*
Palacio	Palace	*Palau*
Paseo	Boulevard	*Passeig*
Pasaje	Passageway	*Passatge*
Plaza	Square	*Plaça*

The maps in this book were prepared by Falk-Verlag, Hamburg, that also publish a detailed map of Barcelona.

I'd like a street plan of...	**Quisiera un plano de la ciudad de...**
a road map of this region	**un mapa de carreteras de esta comarca**

MEDICAL CARE. By far the best solution, to be completely at ease, is to take out a special health insurance policy to cover the risk of illness and accident while on holiday. Your travel agent can also fix you up with Spanish tourist insurance (ASTES), but it is a slow-moving process. ASTES covers doctors' fees and clinical care.

Health care in the resort areas and in the major cities is good but expensive, hence the need for adequate insurance. Most of the major resort towns have private clinics; the cities and rural areas are served by municipal or provincial hospitals.

For minor ailments, visit the local first-aid post *(casa de socorro* or *dispensario).* Away from your hotel, don't hesitate to ask the police or a tourist information office for help. At your hotel, ask the staff to help you.

Pharmacies *(farmacia)* are usually open during normal shopping hours. After hours, at least one per town remains open all night, the *farmacia de guardia.* Its location is posted in the window of all other *farmacias.*

Where's the nearest (all-night) pharmacy?	¿**Donde está la farmacia (de guardia) más cercana?**
I need a doctor/dentist.	**Necesito un médico/dentista.**
I've a pain here.	**Me duele aquí.**
a fever	**fiebre**
sunburn	**quemadura del sol**
an upset stomach	**molestias de estómago**

M **MEETING PEOPLE.** Politeness and simple courtesies still matter in Spain. A handshake on greeting and leaving is normal. Always begin any conversation, whether with a friend, shop girl, taxi-driver, policeman or telephone operator with a *buenos días* (good morning) or *buenas tardes* (good afternoon). Always say *adiós* (good-bye) or, at night, *buenas noches* when leaving. *Por favor* (please) should begin all requests.

Incidentally if anyone should say *adiós* to you when seeing you in the street, it's not that they don't want to have anything to do with you—it's a familiar greeting, meaning roughly "hello".

The Spanish have their own pace. Not only is it bad manners to try to rush them, but unproductive as well.

Outrageous flattery and persistence from complete strangers is the local tactic on the Costa Dorada, a harmless one. But if you're firm and aloof, your admirer will move off.

MONEY MATTERS

Currency. The monetary unit of Spain is the *peseta* (abbreviated *pta.*), which technically is divided into 100 *céntimos*.

Coins: 1, 5, 25 and 50 pesetas.

Banknotes: 100, 500, 1,000 and 5,000 pesetas.

A 5-peseta coin is traditionally called a *duro*, so if someone should quote a price as 10 duros, he means 50 pesetas. For currency restrictions, see ENTRY AND CUSTOMS FORMALITIES.

Banking hours are from 9 a.m. to 2 p.m. Monday to Friday, till 1 p.m. on Saturdays.

Banks are closed on Sundays and holidays—watch out, too, for those local holidays which always seem to crop up in Spain! Outside normal banking hours, many travel agencies and other businesses displaying a *cambio* sign will change foreign currency into pesetas. The exchange rate is a bit less favourable than in the banks. Both banks and exchange offices pay slightly more for traveller's cheques than for cash. Always take your passport with you when you go to exchange money.

Credits cards. The credit card system is a concept new to Spain. Diner's Club and American Express are the most widely accepted cards. Although many hotels, restaurants and tourist-related businesses accept credit cards, Spaniards generally place much more trust in
116 cash. This is particularly so in smaller towns and villages.

Traveller's cheques. In tourist areas, shops and all banks, hotels and travel agencies accept them, though you're likely to get a better exchange rate at a national or regional bank. Remember always to take your passport with you if you expect to cash a traveller's cheque.

Paying cash. Although many shops and bars will accept payment in sterling or dollars, you're better off paying in pesetas. Shops will invariably give you less than the bank rate for foreign currency.

Prices. Although Spain has by no means escaped the scourge of inflation, the Costa Dorada remains quite competitive with the other tourist regions of Europe. An exciting night on the town—either at a discotheque or a flamenco nightclub—won't completely ruin you. In the realm of eating, drinking and smoking, Spain still provides indisputable value for money.

Certain rates are listed on page 101 to give you an idea of what things cost.

Where's the nearest bank/ currency exchange office?	**¿Dónde está el banco/la oficina de cambio más cercana?**
I want to change some pounds/ dollars.	**Quiero cambiar libras/dólares.**
Do you accept traveller's cheques/ Can I pay with this credit card?	**¿Acepta usted cheques de viaje?** **¿Puedo pagar con esta tarjeta de crédito?**
How much is that?	**¿Cuánto es?**

MOSQUITOES. With the occasional exception there are rarely more than a few mosquitoes at a given time, but they survive the year round, and just one can ruin a night's sleep. Few hotels, flats or villas—anywhere on the Mediterranean—have mosquito-proofed windows. Bring your own anti-mosquito devices, whether nets, buzzers, lotions, sprays or incense-type coils that burn all night.

NEWSPAPERS and MAGAZINES *(periódicos; revista)*. At the height of the tourist season, all major British and Continental newspapers are on sale up and down the coast on their publication day. U.S. magazines and the Paris-based *International Herald Tribune* are also available.

Ten daily Spanish-language newspapers are published in Barcelona.

Have you any English-language newspapers/magazines?	**¿Tienen periódicos/revistas en inglés?**

P **PHOTOGRAPHY.** There's tremendous scope for the keen photographer, but beware of the light. For beaches, whitewashed houses and other strongly lit scenes, use incidental readings stopped down, i.e. reduced by one-third or one-half stop; or follow the instructions with the film. If in doubt, bracket your exposures—expose above and below the selected exposure—especially with transparency film. For good results don't shoot between 11 a.m. and 3 p.m. unless there's light cloud to soften the sun.

All popular brands and most sizes of film (except 220) are available. Imported films and chemicals are expensive, so bring as much as you can with you (see ENTRY AND CUSTOMS FORMALITIES).

Spanish-made film is much less expensive and of a reasonable quality. To get best results from the black-and-white *Negra* and *Valca*, you'll need to experiment, especially with processing. The colour negative film *Negracolor* is fine for family shots. All transparency film is imported.

Shops in major resorts usually provide a reasonably priced 48- or 72-hour processing service for both black-and-white and colour. In the summer, films sent to laboratories may take a week or ten days. It's often safer to develop them at home. If possible always keep film—exposed and unexposed—in a refrigerator.

Photos shops sell lead-coated plastic bags which protect films from X-rays at airport security checkpoints.

I'd like a film for this camera.	**Quisiera un carrete para esta máquina.**
a black-and-white film	**un carrete en blanco y negro**
a colour-slide film	**un carrete de diapositivas**
a film for colour-pictures	**un carrete para película en color**
35-mm film	**un carrete treinta y cinco**
super-8	**super ocho**
How long will it take to develop (and print) this film?	**¿Cuánto tardará en revelar (y sacar copias de) este carrete?**

POLICE *(policía).* There are three police forces in Spain: the *Policía Municipal,* who are attached to the local town hall and usually wear a blue uniform; the *Policía Nacional,* a national anti-crime unit recognized by their brown uniforms and black berets; and the *Guardia Civil,* the national police force wearing patent-leather hats, patrolling highways as well as towns.

If you need police assistance, you can call on any one of the three. **P**
Spanish police are efficient, strict and particularly courteous to foreign
visitors.

Where's the nearest police station?	**¿Dónde está la comisaría más cercana?**	

PUBLIC HOLIDAYS *(fiesta)*

January 1	*Año Nuevo*	New Year's Day
January 6	*Epifanía*	Epiphany
May 1	*Día del Trabajo*	Labour Day
July 25	*Santiago Apóstol*	St. James' Day
August 15	*Asunción*	Assumption
October 12	*Día de la Hispanidad*	Discovery of America Day (Columbus Day)
December 8	*Inmaculada Concepción*	Immaculate Conception
December 25	*Navidad*	Christmas Day
Movable dates:	*Jueves Santo*	Maundy Thursday (afternoon only)
	Viernes Santo	Good Friday
	Corpus Christi	Corpus Christi

These are only the national holidays of Spain. There are many special
holidays for different branches of the economy or different regions.
Consult the tourist office where you are staying.

Are you open tomorrow?	**¿Está abierto mañana?**

RADIO and TV *(radio; televisón)*. A short-wave set of reasonable **R**
quality will pick up all European capitals. Reception of Britain's BBC
World Service usually rates from good to excellent, either direct or
through their eastern Mediterranean relay station. In the winter, especially mornings and evenings, a good set will pull in the BBC medium
and long wave "home" programmes. The Voice of America usually
comes through loud and clear, though in Spain the programme is not
received 24 hours a day. The Spanish music programme, *segundo pro-
grama*, jazz to Bach but mostly classical, is excellent. It's FM only,
around 88 UKW on the band.

R Most hotels and bars have television, usually tuned in to sports—including international soccer and rugby—bull fighting, variety or nature programmes. Colour is increasingly used.

RELIGIOUS SERVICES *[servicio religioso].* The national religion of Spain is Roman Catholic. Masses are said regularly in almost all churches, including those of outstanding artistic or historical interest. In principal tourist centres, Catholic services are also held in foreign languages. In Barcelona, Sunday mass in English is said at the parish church of Santa María de la Bonanova, Plaza de la Bonanova, 12. In Barcelona Cathedral confessions are heard each Sunday in English.

Protestant services for English-speaking foreigners in Barcelona: St. George's Anglican Church, Calle Juan Bautista de la Salle, 41 (near Plaza de la Bonanova). In Castelldefels, Protestant services are held once a month in the parish church.

Jewish service: Barcelona Synagogue, Calle Porvenir, 24.

What time is mass/the service?	**¿A qué hora es la misa/el culto?**
Is it in English?	**¿Es en inglés?**

T **TIMES DIFFERENCES.** Spanish time coincides with most of Western Europe—Greenwich Mean Time plus on hour. In spring, another hour is added for Daylight Saving Time (Summer Time).

Summer Time chart:

New York	London	**Spain**	Jo'burg	Sydney	Auckland
6 a.m.	11 a.m.	**noon**	noon	8 p.m.	10 p.m.

What time is it? **¿Qué hora es?**

TIPPING. Since a service charge is normally included in hotel and restaurant bills, tipping is not obligatory. However, it's appropriate to tip porters, bellboys, etc., for their efforts.

Follow the chart below for rough guidelines.

Hotel porter, per bag	25 ptas.
Bellboy, errand	50 ptas.
Maid, per week	100 ptas.

Doorman, hails cab	25 ptas.
Waiter	10–12%, if service not incl.
Taxi driver	10%
Filling station attendant	25 ptas., optional
Tourist guide	10%
Hairdresser	10%
Cinema usher	10–15 ptas.
Bullfight usher	10–15 ptas.
Lavatory attendant	10–15 ptas.

TOILETS. There are many expressions for "toilets" in Spanish: *aseos, servicios., W.C., water* and *retretes.* The first terms are the more common.

Public toilets are to be found in most large towns, but rarely in villages. However, just about every bar and restaurant has a toilet available for public use. It's considered polite to buy a coffee or a glass of wine if you drop in specifically to use the conveniences.

Where are the toilets?	**¿Dónde están los servicios?**

TOURIST INFORMATION OFFICES *(oficinas de turismo).* Spanish National Tourist Offices are maintained in many countries throughout the world:

Canada. 60 Bloor St. West, Suite 201, Toronto, Ont. M4W-3B8; tel. (416) 961-3131

United Kingdom. 57–58, St. James's St., London SW1 A1LD; tel. (01) 499-1095.

U.S.A. 845 N. Michigan Ave., Chicago, IL 60611; tel. (312) 944-0215.

665 5th Ave., New York, NY 10022; tel. (212) 759-8822.

Casa del Hidalgo, Hypolita & St. George Streets, St. Augustine, FL 31084; tel. (904) 829-6460.

1 Hallidie Plaza, Suite 801, San Francisco, CA 94102; tel. (415) 346-8100.

Fortaleza 367, P.O. Box 463, San Juan, P.R. 00902; tel. 725-0625. **121**

These offices will supply you with a wide range of colourful and informative brochures and maps in English on the various towns and regions in Spain. They will also let you consult a copy of the master directory of hotels in Spain, listing all facilities and prices.

All major cities and leading resorts in Spain have their own tourist information offices, all of which will be delighted to provide information and brochures on local tourist attractions.

Barcelona. Gran Vía, 658; tel. 301-74-43

Sitges. Plaza Eduardo Maristany; tel. 894-12-30.

Tarragona. Rambla Nova, 46; tel. 20-1859.

Where is the tourist office?   **¿Dónde está la oficina de turismo?**

TRANSPORT

Buses. More than 50 bus lines cover Barcelona. As in many cities, the rush hours are best avoided.

Most buses are boarded by the rear door; a conductor at a little counter just inside issues tickets. Automatic ticket machines are being introduced that require the exact fare.

To reach the resorts from Barcelona, trains are more frequent and practical than the bus services.

Metro*. Barcelona's underground railway, consisting of five main lines, criss-crosses the city more rapidly than other forms of public transport. However, some trains are old and dingy and, in summer, the ride can be mercilessly hot and humid.

"Metro" signs with a red diamond-shaped insignia mark the entrances where detailed maps of all lines are displayed. Trains run from 5 a.m. to 11 p.m.

Taxis*. You can recognize taxis by the letters SP *(servicio público)* on the front and rear bumpers. They may also have a green light on the roof and a *libre* (free) sign on the windscreen. Each town has its own type of car and colour scheme (Barcelona's 9,000 taxis are all painted yellow and black). In smaller towns, there are fixed fares instead of meters; in major cities, the meter clicks relentlessly as you go. The figure displayed at the end of your trip probably is not the full fare—the driver carries an official list giving the correct total, adjusted upwards for inflation. Additional charges are legitimately made for any number of circumstances—such as nights and holidays, or picking you up at a railway station, airport, theatre or bullring. Whatever the total, it usually still costs less than a comparable journey in many other European countries.

Trains. From Barcelona, main line trains reach to most corners of Spain. Local trains are slow, stopping at most stations. Long-distance services are fast and punctual. First-class coaches are comfortable; second-class, adequate; third class, when available, uncomfortable but cheap. Tickets can be purchased at travel agencies as well as at the stations *(estación de ferrocarril)*. For long trips, seat reservations are recommended.

Trains to resorts north-east of Barcelona use the Cercanías station, a separate installation behind the main Estación de Francia. Suburban trains to the south-west sometimes run from the Paseo de Gracia station in the centre of town.

Talgo, Ter	Luxury diesel, first and second classes; supplementary charge over regular fare
Expreso, Rápido	Long-distance expresses, stopping at main stations only
Omnibus, Tranvía, Automotor	Local trains, with frequent stops
coche cama	Sleeping-car with 1-, 2- or 3-bed compartments, washing facilities
coche comedor	Dining-car
litera	Sleeping-berth car *(couchette)* with blankets, sheets and pillows
furgón de equipajes	Luggage van (baggage car); only registered luggage permitted

When's the next bus/train to…?	**¿Cuándo sale el próximo autobús/ tren para…?**
single (one-way)	**ida**
return (round-trip)	**ida y vuelta**
What's the fare to…?	**¿Cuánto es la tarifa a…?**
first/second/third class	**primera/segunda/tercera clase**
I'd like to make seat reservations.	**Quiero reservar asientos.**
Where can I get a taxi?	**¿Dónde puedo coger un taxi?**

WATER *(agua)* When Spaniards drink water, it is almost invariably bottled, rather than from the tap. It is quite common to order water brought to one's room. Water varies enormously in taste and quality; the bottled variety is good, pure and cheap.

a bottle of mineral water	**una botella de agua mineral**
fizzy (carbonated)	**con gas**
still (non-carbonated)	**sin gas**
Is this drinking water?	**¿El agua es potable?**

DAYS OF THE WEEK

Sunday	**domingo**	Thursday	**jueves**
Monday	**lunes**	Friday	**viernes**
Tuesday	**martes**	Saturday	**sábado**
Wednesday	**miércoles**		

NUMBERS

0	**cero**	18	**dieciocho**
1	**uno**	19	**diecinueve**
2	**dos**	20	**veinte**
3	**tres**	21	**veintiuno**
4	**cuatro**	22	**veintidós**
5	**cinco**	30	**treinta**
6	**seis**	31	**treinta y uno**
7	**siete**	32	**treinta y dos**
8	**ocho**	40	**cuarenta**
9	**nueve**	50	**cincuenta**
10	**diez**	60	**sesenta**
11	**once**	70	**setenta**
12	**doce**	80	**ochenta**
13	**trece**	90	**noventa**
14	**catorce**	100	**cien**
15	**quince**	101	**cientouno**
16	**dieciséis**	500	**quinientos**
17	**diecisiete**	1,000	**mil**

SOME USEFUL EXPRESSIONS

yes/no	**sí/no**
please/thank you	**por favor/gracias**
excuse me/you're welcome	**perdone/de nada**
where/when/how	**dónde/cuándo/cómo**
how long/how far	**cuánto tiempo/a qué distancia**
yesterday/today/tomorrow	**ayer/hoy/mañana**
day/week/month/year	**día/semana/mes/año**
left/right	**izquierda/derecha**
up/down	**arriba/abajo**
good/bad	**bueno/malo**
big/small	**grande/pequeño**
cheap/expensive	**barato/caro**
hot/cold	**caliente/frío**
old/new	**viejo/nuevo**
open/closed	**abierto/cerrado**
here/there	**aquí/allí**
free (vacant)/occupied	**libre/ocupado**
early/late	**temprano/tarde**
easy/difficult	**fácil/difícil**

Does anyone here speak English?	**¿Hay alguien aquí que hable inglés?**
What does this mean?	**¿Qué quiere decir esto?**
I don't understand.	**No comprendo.**
Please write it down.	**Por favor, escríbalo.**
Is there an admission charge?	**¿Se debe pagar la entrada?**
Waiter!/Waitress!	**¡Camarero!/¡Camarera!**
I'd like...	**Quisiera...**
How much is that?	**¿Cuánto es?**
Have you something less expensive?	**¿Tiene algo más barato?**
Just a minute.	**Un momento.**
Help me, please.	**Ayúdeme, por favor.**
get a doctor, quickly.	**¡Llamen a un médico, rápidamente!**

Index

An asterisk (*) next to a page number indicates a map reference.

INDEX

127

INDEX